U.S. Presbyterian Church

Missionary Exercises for the use of Sunday-Schools and Mission-Bands

consisting of responsive readings, dialogues, selections in prose and poetry etc.

U.S. Presbyterian Church

Missionary Exercises for the use of Sunday-Schools and Mission-Bands
consisting of responsive readings, dialogues, selections in prose and poetry etc.

ISBN/EAN: 9783337369224

Printed in Europe, USA, Canada, Australia, Japan

Cover: Foto ©Lupo / pixelio.de

More available books at **www.hansebooks.com**

Missionary Exercises

FOR THE USE OF

Sunday-Schools and Mission-Bands

CONSISTING OF

RESPONSIVE READINGS, DIALOGUES, SELECTIONS
IN PROSE AND POETRY, Etc.

ARRANGED BY

THE WOMAN'S FOREIGN MISSIONARY SOCIETY OF
THE PRESBYTERIAN CHURCH

———

PHILADELPHIA
PRESBYTERIAN BOARD OF PUBLICATION
No. 1334 CHESTNUT STREET

CONTENTS.

	PAGE
Responsive Readings..	5
Illustrative Band-Meeting.....................................	32
List of Subjects for Meetings...............................	36
Missionary Map-Making..	40
Illustrations for Item-Gatherers........................	44
Dialogues and Exercises in Prose and Poetry......	48
Poems for Recitation or Singing...........................	138

MISSIONARY EXERCISES.

RESPONSIVE READINGS.

No. 1. RESPONSIVE BIBLE-READING.

Leader.—Sing praises to God, sing praises; sing praises unto our King, sing praises.

Band.—For God is the King of all the earth, sing ye praises with understanding.

L.—God reigneth over the heathen. God sitteth upon the throne of his holiness.

B.—God be merciful unto us, and bless us; and cause his face to shine upon us.

L.—That thy way may be known upon earth; thy saving health among all nations.

B.—Let the people praise thee, O God, let all the people praise thee.

L.—Let all the nations be glad and sing for joy; for thou shalt judge the people righteously, and govern the nations upon earth.

B.—That all the people of the earth may know that the Lord is God, and there is none else.

L.—Then shall the earth yield her increase, and God, even our own God, shall bless us.

B.—God shall bless us, and all the ends of the earth shall fear him.

L.—Be still, and know that I am God; I will be

exalted among the heathen, I will be exalted in the earth.

B.—Go ye into all the world, and preach the gospel to every creature.

All.—Lo, I am with you alway, even unto the end of the world.

No. 2. MISSION-WORK IN THE BIBLE.

COMMANDS.

[These texts are to be recited by the classes in order, or read alternately by the leader and the school.]

Therefore said he unto them, The harvest truly *is* great, but the laborers *are* few: pray ye therefore the Lord of the harvest, that he would send forth laborers into his harvest. Luke 10:2.

In the morning sow thy seed, and in the evening withhold not thy hand: for thou knowest not whether shall prosper, either this or that, or whether they both *shall be* alike good. Eccles. 11:6.

Say among the heathen *that* the LORD reigneth: the world also shall be established that it shall not be moved: he shall judge the people righteously. Ps. 96:10.

Honor the LORD with thy substance, and with the first-fruits of all thine increase. Prov. 3:9.

Declare his glory among the heathen, his wonders among all people. Ps. 96:3.

Go through, go through the gates; prepare ye the way of the people; cast up, cast up the highway; gather out the stones; lift up a standard for the people. Isa. 62:10.

And heal the sick that are therein, and say unto

them, The kingdom of God is come nigh unto you. Luke 10 : 9.

And Jesus said unto them, Come ye after me, and I will make you to become fishers of men. Mark 1 : 17.

Go ye therefore, and teach all nations, baptizing them in the name of the Father, and of the Son, and of the Holy Ghost.

Teaching them to observe all things whatsoever I have commanded you: and lo, I am with you always, *even* unto the end of the world. Amen. Matt. 28 : 19, 20.

That repentance and remission of sins should be preached in his name among all nations, beginning at Jerusalem. Luke 24 : 47.

And he commanded us to preach unto the people, and to testify that it is he which was ordained of God *to be* the Judge of quick and dead. Acts 10 : 42.

I have showed you all things, how that so laboring ye ought to support the weak, and to remember the words of the Lord Jesus, how he said, It is more blessed to give than to receive. Acts 20 : 35.

Every man according as he purposeth in his heart, *so let him give;* not grudgingly, or of necessity · for God loveth a cheerful giver. 2 Cor. 9 : 7.

ENCOURAGEMENTS.

Fear thou not; for I *am* with thee: be not dismayed; for I am thy God: I will strengthen thee; yea, I will help thee; yea, I will uphold thee with the right hand of my righteousness. Isa. 41 : 10.

And I will bring the blind by a way *that* they knew not; I will lead them in paths *that* they have not known: I will make darkness light before them, and crooked things straight. These things will I do unto them, and not forsake them. Isa. 42:16.

Thou therefore gird up thy loins, and arise, and speak unto them all that I command thee: be not dismayed at their faces, lest I confound thee before them. Jer. 1:17.

And the idols he shall utterly abolish. Isa. 2:18.

They shall not hurt nor destroy in all my holy mountain: for the earth shall be full of the knowledge of the Lord, as the waters cover the sea. Isa. 11:9.

Fear not; for I *am* with thee: I will bring thy seed from the east, and gather them from the west. Isa. 43:5.

They shall lift up their voice, they shall sing for the majesty of the Lord, they shall cry aloud from the sea. Isa. 24:14.

REWARDS.

Cast thy bread upon the waters: for thou shalt find it after many days. Eccles. 11:1.

And they that be wise shall shine as the brightness of the firmament; and they that turn many to righteousness, as the stars for ever and ever. Dan. 12:3.

And when the chief Shepherd shall appear, ye shall receive a crown of glory that fadeth not away. 1 Pet. 5:4.

For he that soweth to his flesh shall of the flesh reap corruption; but he that soweth to the Spirit, shall of the Spirit reap life everlasting. Gal. 6:8.

The liberal soul shall be made fat; and he that watereth shall be watered also himself. Prov. 11:25.

Primary Class.—

The idols of the heathen *are* silver and gold, the work of men's hands.

They have mouths, but they speak not; eyes have they, but they see not;

They have ears, but they hear not; neither is there *any* breath in their mouths.

They that make them are like unto them; *so is* every one that trusteth in them. Ps. 135 : 15, 16, 17, 18.

FINAL GLORY.

How beautiful upon the mountains are the feet of him that bringeth good tidings, that publisheth peace; that bringeth good tidings of good, that publisheth salvation: that saith unto Zion, Thy God reigneth! Isa. 52 : 7.

Thy people also *shall be* all righteous: they shall inherit the land for ever, the branch of my planting, the work of my hands, that I may be glorified.

A little one shall become a thousand, and a small one a strong nation: I the Lord will hasten it in his time. Isa. 60 : 21, 22.

Thou shalt also be a crown of glory in the hand of the Lord, and a royal diadem in the hand of thy God. Isa. 62 : 3.

And it shall come to pass in the last days, *that* the mountain of the Lord's house shall be established in the top of the mountains, and shall be exalted above the hills; and all nations shall flow into it. Isa. 2 : 2.

No. 3. PROMISES OF CHRIST'S UNIVERSAL REIGN.

Ps. 22 : 27-31; Ps. 68 : 31; Isa. 2 : 2, 3; Isa 25 : 7, 8; Isa. 66 : 23, 24; Jer. 4 : 2; Mic. 4 : 1, 2; Heb. 2 : 14; Matt. 16 : 18, 19; Heb. 8 : 11; Rev. 14 : 6.

No. 4. THE BLESSEDNESS OF GIVING.

Mark 12 : 41-44; 1 Tim. 6 : 17-19; Rom. 11 : 35, 36; 1 Chron. 29 : 9-16; John 3 : 16; Matt. 5 : 42.

No. 5. CHRIST'S DOMINION.

Leader.—Every valley shall be filled, and every mountain and hill shall be brought low; and the crooked shall be made straight, and the rough ways shall be made smooth.

School.—And all flesh shall see the salvation of God.

Teachers.—This is he of whom it is written, Behold I send my messenger before thy face, which shall prepare thy way before thee.

S.—The voice of him that crieth in the wilderness, Prepare ye the way of the Lord, make straight in the desert a highway for our God.

L.—And the glory of the Lord shall be revealed, and all flesh shall see it together:

T.—For the mouth of the Lord hath spoken it.

S.—He shall have dominion also from sea to sea, and from the river to the ends of the earth.

T.—They that dwell in the wilderness shall bow before him; and his enemies shall lick the dust.

L.—Yea, all kings shall fall down before him; all nations shall serve him.

S.—Ask of me, and I shall give thee the heathen for thine inheritance, and the uttermost parts of the earth for thy possession.

L.—All the ends of the world shall remember, and turn unto the Lord.

T.—And all the kindreds of the nations shall worship before thee.

L.—Princes shall come out of Egypt: Ethiopia shall soon stretch out her hands unto God.

S.—My righteousness is near; my salvation is gone forth, and mine arms shall judge the people: the isles shall wait upon me, and on mine arm shall they trust,

L.—And the Gentiles shall see thy righteousness, and all kings thy glory. . . .

S.—And many nations shall come, and say, Come, and let us go up to the mountain of the Lord, and to the house of the God of Jacob; and he will teach us of his ways, and we will walk in his paths; for the law shall go forth of Zion, and the word of the Lord from Jerusalem.

L.—And they shall come from the east, and from the west, and from the north, and from the south, and shall sit down in the kingdom of God.

S.—And there were great voices in heaven, saying, The kingdoms of this world are become the kingdoms of our Lord, and of his Christ; and he shall reign for ever and ever.

L.—Give, and it shall be given unto you; good measure, pressed down, and shaken together, and running over, shall men give into your bosom. For with the same measure that ye mete withal, it shall be measured to you again.

S.—Cast thy bread upon the waters, for thou shalt find it after many days.

L.—He that hath two coats, let him impart to him that hath none; and he that hath meat, let him do likewise.

S.—He that goeth forth and weepeth, bearing precious seed, shall doubtless come again with rejoicing, bringing his sheaves with him.

L.—But the liberal deviseth liberal things, and by liberal things shall he stand.

S.—That they do good, that they be rich in good works, ready to distribute, willing to communicate.

L.—I have showed you all things, how that so laboring ye ought to support the weak; and to remember the words of the Lord Jesus, how he said, It is more blessed to give than to receive.

S.—Lift up your eyes and look on the fields, for they are white already to harvest.

L.—But this I say, He which soweth sparingly shall reap also sparingly; and he which soweth bountifully shall reap also bountifully.

S.—Every man according as he purposeth in his heart, so let him give; not grudgingly or of necessity; for God loveth a cheerful giver.

L.—Thy kingdom come, thy will be done, in earth as it is in heaven.

S.—Now He that ministereth seed to the sower, both minister bread for your food, and multiply your seed sown, and increase the fruits of your righteousness.

L.—And if thou draw out thy soul to the hungry, and satisfy the afflicted soul; then shall thy light rise in obscurity, and thy darkness be as the noonday.

S.—Withhold not good from them to whom it is due, when it is in the power of thine hand to do it.

L.—Say not unto thy neighbor, Go and come again, and to-morrow I will give; when thou hast it by thee.

S.—Therefore as ye abound in everything, . . . see that ye abound in this grace also, . . . for ye know the grace of our Lord Jesus Christ, that though he was rich, yet for your sakes he became poor, that ye through his poverty might be rich.

L.—There is that scattereth, and yet increaseth; and

there is that withholdeth more than is meet, but it tendeth to poverty.

S.—The liberal soul shall be made fat; and he that watereth shall be watered also himself.

L.—Upon the first day of the week let every one of you lay by him in store, as God hath prospered him, that there be no gatherings when I come.

S.—The harvest truly is great, but the laborers are few; pray ye therefore the Lord of the harvest, that he would send forth laborers into his harvest.

L.—This gospel of the kingdom shall be preached in all the world, for a witness unto all nations.

S.—And when I come, whomsoever ye shall approve by your letters, them will I send to bring your liberality unto Jerusalem.

L.—And whosoever shall give to drink unto one of these little ones a cup of cold water only in the name of a disciple, verily I say unto you, he shall in no wise lose his reward.

S.—And let us not be weary in well-doing; for in due season we shall reap if we faint not.

L.—Declare his glory among the heathen, his wonders among all people.

S.—Oh send out thy light and thy truth, . . . that thy way may be known upon the earth, thy saving health among all nations.

L.—The dark places of the earth are full of the habitations of cruelty.

S.—As we have therefore opportunity, let us do good unto all men.

No. 6. THE WORD AND THE WORK.

1. *What is the great commission?*

And he said unto them, Go ye into all the world, and preach the gospel to every creature.

2. *Who were the first missionaries, and by whom appointed?*

As they ministered to the Lord, and fasted, the Holy Ghost said, Separate me Barnabas and Saul for the work whereunto I have called them.

3. *Is the field ready for the harvest?*

Behold I say unto you, Lift up your eyes, and look on the fields, for they are white already to harvest.

4. *Are the heathen condemned?*

Wherefore as by man sin entered into the world, and death by sin, so death passed upon all men, for that all have sinned.

5. *Have they any excuse for not believing?*

For the invisible things of him from the creation of the world are clearly seen, being understood by the things that are made, even his eternal power and Godhead: so that they are without excuse.

6. *How, then, can the heathen be saved?*

And the Scripture, foreseeing that God would justify the heathen through faith, preached before the gospel unto Abraham, saying, In thee shall all nations be blessed.

7. *Is there salvation for them excepting through Christ?*

Neither is there salvation in any other, for there is none other name under heaven given among men whereby we must be saved.

8. *How can they obtain faith?*

So then faith cometh by hearing, and hearing by the word of God.

9. *What plea, then, can the heathen bring for their unbelief?*

How then shall they call on Him in whom they have not believed? And how shall they believe in Him of whom they have not heard? And how shall they hear without a preacher?

10. *Have we reason to believe that missions to the heathen will be crowned with success?*

Ask of me, and I shall give thee the heathen for thine inheritance, and the uttermost parts of the earth for thy possession.

11. *Is it God's purpose that the gospel should be preached to all nations?*

Thus it is written, and thus it behooved Christ to suffer, and to rise from the dead the third day: and that repentance and remission of sins should be preached in his name among all nations, beginning at Jerusalem.

12. *Is it still right and necessary to pray for the accomplishment of this purpose?*

Thus saith the Lord God, I will yet for this be inquired of by the house of Israel to do it for them. Pray ye therefore the Lord of the harvest, that he will send forth laborers into his harvest.

13. *What promise of assistance have we in this work?*

Teaching them to observe all things whatsoever I have commanded you, and lo, I am with you alway, even unto the end of the world?

14. *When shall the end come?*

And this gospel of the kingdom shall be preached in all the world for a witness unto all nations, and then shall the end come.

No. 7. OPENING EXERCISE.

Leader.—We beseech thee, O God of hosts; look down from heaven, and behold, and visit this vine and the vineyard which thy right hand hath planted, and the branch which thou madest strong for thyself. Ps. 80: 14, 15.

Reply, by member of the Band.—I will pour water upon him that is thirsty, and floods upon the dry grounds. I will pour my Spirit upon thy seed and my blessing upon thine offspring; and they shall spring up as among the grass, as willows by the water-courses. One shall say, I am the Lord's; and another shall call himself by the name of Jacob; and another shall subscribe with his hand unto the Lord, and surname himself by the name of Jacob. Isa. 44: 3–5.

L.—What shall we then say to these things? If God be for us, who can be against us? Rom. 8: 31.

R.—Fear thou not, for I am with thee; be not dismayed; for I am thy God; I will strengthen thee; yea, I will help thee; yea, I will uphold thee with the right hand of my righteousness. Isa. 41: 10.

L.—God is not a man, that he should lie; neither the son of man, that he should repent: hath he said, and shall he not do it? or hath he spoken, and shall he not make it good? Num. 23: 19.

R.—And behold, this day I am going the way of all the earth: and ye know in all your hearts and in all your souls, that not one thing hath failed of all the good things which the Lord your God spake concerning you; all are come to pass unto you, and not one thing hath failed thereof. Josh. 23: 14.

L.—What shall I render unto the Lord for all his benefits toward me? Ps. 16: 12.

R.—And he said unto them, Go ye into all the world and preach the gospel to every creature (Mark 16 : 15). Let your light so shine before men that they may see your good works, and glorify your Father which is in heaven. Matt. 5 : 16.

No. 8. PAUL'S MISSIONARY JOURNEYS.

[Let the following exercise be illustrated by maps, diagrams and pictures, and clearly explained by the Superintendent. By taking the journeys separately, and interspersing singing and other exercises, each may be made the subject of an entire meeting.]

RECITATIONS.

I. *The Gentile Church at Antioch.* Acts 11 : 19–28.

II. *Paul's First Missionary Journey.*

Cyprus and Perga. Acts 13 : 4–14.
Antioch in Pisidia. Acts 13 : 44–49.
Iconium. Acts 13 : 49–52; 14 : 1–3.
Lystra and Derbe. Acts 14 : 4–20.
Antioch. Acts 14 : 21–28.

A. D. 46–47.

III. *Paul's Second Missionary Journey.* Acts 15 : 36.

Syria and Asia Minor. Acts 15 : 40, 41 ; 16 : 1–5.
Europe. Acts 16 : 11–13.
Athens. Acts 17 : 15 ; 17 : 16–21.
Sermon at Athens. Acts 17 : 22–34.
At Corinth. Acts 18 : 1–6 ; 18 : 7–11.

A. D. 51–54.

IV. *Paul's Third Misionary Tour.* Acts 18 : 21–23.

Ephesus. Acts 19 : 1–7.

A. D. 54–57.

Greece. Acts 20 : 1–3.
Troas. Acts 20 : 6, 7.
Miletus. Acts 20 : 17–23.

V. *Paul's Fourth Missionary Tour.*

Italy. Acts 27.

[Let this journey be narrated by the Superintendent and shown by pictures and diagrams.]

Rome. Acts 28 : 12–16.

Supt.—What cities have been mentioned in Paul's missionary tours?

Supt.—After Paul had established churches in these cities, how did he continue to instruct and guide them?

School.—By letters or Epistles.

Supt.—Repeat the beginning of Paul's letter to the Romans.

Pupil.—Rom. 1 : 1–7.

Supt.—Where was this letter written, and by whom was it sent?

Acts 16 (paragraphic note).

Supt.—Repeat the salutation to the Corinthians in Paul's first letter.

1 Cor. 1 : 1–3.

Supt.—Where were the letters to the Corinthians written? (At Philippi.)

Supt.—Repeat Paul's benediction in his letter to the Ephesians.

Eph. 6 : 23, 24.

Supt.—Where was the letter to the Ephesians written? (Rome.)

Supt.—Repeat Paul's impressive charge to the Thessalonians. 1 Thess. 5 : 14–28.

Supt.—Where was the letter written? (Athens.)

An address may appropriately follow, showing how

the gospel, after the decease of the apostles, spread over Europe, and its present progress in the world.

[Used by special permission of Garrigues Brothers, Philadelphia, who publish the exercises in tract form.]

No. 9. THE WHITE ROBE.

Sing, "Around the throne of God in heaven," etc.

Read, Ecclesiastes 9.

How can we have this robe here on earth? Isa. 61 : 10.

How are we told to keep our garments? Eccles. 9 : 8.

How do we soil our garments?

How can we have them made clean? Ps. 51 : 2, 7.

Sing, "All to Christ I owe."

Will we have white robes in heaven? Rev. 7 : 9.

How shall we get them? Rev. 7 : 14.

Sing, "Jesus the water of life will give," 3d verse.

What are we commanded to do? Rev. 16 : 15.

If we keep our robes clean here on earth, what will Christ say to us at the last day? Song of Sol. 4 : 7.

RECITATION.

"Heavenly Father, I would wear
  Angel garments white and fair;
  Angel vesture undefiled
Wilt thou give unto thy child.

"Take the raiment soiled away
  That I wear with shame to-day;

Give my angel robes to me,
White with heaven's own purity.

"Take away my cloak of pride,
That the worthless rags would hide
Clothe me in my angel dress,
Beautiful with holiness.

"Let me wear the white robes here,
E'en on earth, my Father dear,
Holding fast thy hand, and so
Through the world unspotted go."
Children's Work for Children.

No. 10. GIVING.

By Mrs. A. E. Penney.

What was God's best gift to man?
God so loved the world, etc. John 3 : 16.
What should be the measure of our giving.
Freely ye have received, freely give. Matt. 10 : 8.
What is first accepted in giving?
If there be first a willing mind, etc. 2 Cor. 8 : 12.
Who should give?
Every man as he purposeth in his heart. 2 Cor. 9 : 7.
To whom should we give?
As we have therefore opportunity, etc. Gal. 6 : 10.
What promise to those who honor God by giving?
Honor the Lord with thy substance, etc. Prov. 3 : 9, 10.
Give and it shall be given you, etc. Luke 6 : 38.
If thou draw out thy soul to the hungry, etc. Isa. 58 : 10, 11.
What did Jesus observe at the temple treasury?

And Jesus sat over against the treasury, etc. Mark 12 : 41, 42.

What was his comment on this act?

And he called unto him his disciples, etc. Mark 12 : 43, 44.

What spirit did David show in making his offering to the Lord?

And the king said unto Araunah, etc. 2 Sam. 24 : 24.

Is it safe to refrain from giving?

There is that withholdeth more than is meet, etc. Prov. 11 : 24.

As God's stewards what is required of us?

Moreover it is required in stewards, etc. 1 Cor. 4 : 2.

To whom do we all belong?

And ye are not your own; for ye are bought with a price, etc. 1 Cor. 6 : 19, 20, last clause; also, 1 Cor. 2 : 23.—*The Missionary Helper.*

No. 11. FAITH, HOPE AND CHARITY.

[A concert exercise for five girls or boys.]

By Mrs. M. B. C. Slade.

In Concert.—And now abideth faith, hope, charity, these three; but the greatest of these is charity. 1 Cor. 13 : 13.

First.—Faith is the substance of things hoped for, the evidence of things not seen. Heb. 11 : 1.

Second.—Without faith it is impossible to please him. Heb. 11 : 6.

Third.—Faith which worketh by love. Gal. 5 : 6.

Fourth.—Faith cometh by hearing, and hearing by the word of God. Rom. 10 : 17.

Fifth.—Fight the good fight of faith; lay hold on eternal life. 1 Tim. 6 : 12.

First.—Abide in me, strong Faith, bright evidence
　Of things beyond the sphere of time and sense;
Be thou the light to gleam our pathway o'er
Till faith is changed to light for evermore.
　Abide in me, strong Faith.

First.—What is our hope, or joy, or crown of rejoicing? 1 Thess. 2 : 19.

Second.—It is good that a man should both hope and quietly wait for the salvation of the Lord. Lam. 3 : 26.

Third.—The hope of the righteous shall be gladness. Prov. 10 : 28.

Fourth.—Happy is he that hath the God of Jacob for his help, whose hope is in the Lord his God. Ps. 146 : 5.

Fifth.—Which hope we have as an anchor of the soul, both sure and steadfast. Heb. 6 : 19.

Second.—Abide in me, calm Hope; on thee we lean
　While journeying onward to the shore unseen—
Thou anchor to the soul that cannot fail,
Which entereth into that within the veil.
　Abide in me, calm Hope.

First.—Above all these things put on charity, which is the bond of perfectness. Col. 3 : 14.

Second.—Be thou an example of the believers in word, in conversation, in charity. 1 Tim. 4 : 12.

Third.—The end of the commandment is charity, out of a pure heart. 1 Tim. 1 : 5.

Fourth.—Though I speak with the tongues of men and of angels, and have not charity, I am become as sounding brass or a tinkling cymbal. 1 Cor. 13 : 1.

Fifth.—And now abideth faith, hope and charity, these three, but the greatest of these is charity. 1 Cor. 13:13.

Third.—Abide in me, pure Charity divine;
Within our hearts and in our actions shine.
'Tis thine to soothe, to cheer, to help, to bless,
Thou crowning grace, bright bond of perfectness.
Abide in me, sweet Charity.

In Concert.—Faith, Hope and Charity, bright gems divine,
In us, as jewels, shine;
Faith, Hope and Charity, each lovely grace
Within our souls have place.
Faith, Hope and Charity—Lord, these shall be
Our guides to heaven and thee.

Good Times.

No. 12. WIDENING PROMISES.

By H. M. J.

[This responsive exercise was written for a class of sixteen young ladies. Eight sat on each side the pulpit, one prominent voice reciting Promise No. 1. Four voices on the opposite side next recited Promise No. 2; then all the voices joined in reciting the last and widest promise with emphasis. Then they began again with No. 1, then No. 2, and so on.]

Promise No. 1.

1. Num. 24:17: There shall come a *star* out of Jacob.

2. Isa. 60:3: *And the Gentiles shall come to thy light, and kings to the brightness of thy rising.*

3. Isa. 49 : 6 : I will also give thee for a light to the Gentiles, that thou mayest be my salvation *unto the end of the earth.*

No. 2.

1. Zech. 13 : 1 : In that day there shall be a fountain opened to the house of David, and to the inhabitants of Jerusalem, for sin and for uncleanness.

2. Ezek. 36 : 25, 26 : *Then will I sprinkle clean water upon you, and ye shall be clean; from all your filthiness, and from all your idols will I cleanse you. A new heart also will I give you, and a new spirit will I put within you.*

3. Heb. 8 : 12 : For I will be merciful to their unrighteousness and their sins, and their iniquities will I remember no more.

No. 3.

1. Luke 2 : 10 : And the angel said unto them, Fear not, for behold, I bring you good tidings of great joy, which shall be to all people.

2. Isa. 9 : 6 : *For unto us a child is born, unto us a son is given; and the government shall be upon his shoulder: and his name shall be called Wonderful, Counselor, the Mighty God, the Everlasting Father, the Prince of Peace.*

3. Luke 1 : 33 : And he shall reign over the house of Jacob *for ever*, and of his kingdom *there shall be no end.*

No. 4.

1. Mal. 3 : 3 : The Lord whom ye seek shall suddenly come to his temple, even the messenger of the covenant, whom ye delight in: behold, he shall come, saith the Lord of hosts.

2. Isa. 55 : 3 : *I will make an everlasting covenant with you, even the sure mercies of David.*

3. Isa. 59 : 21 : This is my covenant with them, saith the Lord; my Spirit that is upon thee, and my words which I have put in thy mouth, shall not

depart out of thy mouth, nor out of the mouth of thy seed, nor out of the mouth of thy seed's seed, saith the Lord, *from henceforth and for ever.*

No. 5.

1. Isa. 40 : 8 : The grass withereth, the flower fadeth : but the word of our God shall stand for ever.

2. Luke 21 : 33 : *Heaven and earth shall pass away, but my words shall not pass away.*

3. Isa. 55 : 10, 11 : For as the rain cometh down, and the snow from heaven, and returneth not thither, but watereth the earth and maketh it bring forth and bud, that it may give seed to the sower and bread to the eater; so shall my word be that goeth forth out of my mouth; it shall not return unto me void, but it shall accomplish that which I please, and it shall prosper in the thing whereto I sent it.

No. 6.

1. Isa. 42 : 17 : They shall be turned back, they shall be greatly ashamed that trust in graven images, that say to the molten images, Ye are our gods.

2. Zech 13 : 2 : *I will cut off the names of the idols out of the land, and they shall no more be remembered.*

3. Mal. 1 : 11 : For from the rising of the sun even unto the going down of the same, my name shall be great among the Gentiles; and in every place incense shall be offered unto my name, and a pure offering; for my name shall be great among the heathen, saith the Lord of hosts.

No. 7.

1. Ezek. 36 : 23 : I will sanctify my great name which was profaned among the heathen, . . . and the heathen shall know that I am the Lord, saith the

Lord God, when I shall be sanctified in you before their eyes.

2. Isa. 43 : 5 : *Fear not, for I am with thee.*

3. Isa. 43 : 6 : I will bring thy seed from the east, and gather thee from the west; I will say to the north, Give up; and to the south, Keep not back, bring my sons from far, and my daughters from the ends of the earth.

No. 8.

1. Acts 1 : 8 : Ye shall receive power after that the Holy Ghost is come upon you, and ye shall be witnesses unto me both in Jerusalem and in all Judæa—

2. *And in Samaria—*

3. And unto the *uttermost part of the earth.*

No. 9.

1. Isa. 45 : 23 : Unto me every knee shall bow, every tongue shall swear.

2. Isa. 40 : 4 : *Every valley shall be exalted, and every mountain and hill shall be made low, and the crooked shall be made straight, and the rough places plain.*

3. And the glory of the Lord shall be revealed, and *all flesh shall see it together.*

No. 10.

1. Matt. 24 : 14 : This gospel of the kingdom shall be preached in all the world for a witness unto all nations.

2. *And then shall the end come.*

3. Dan. 7 : 27 : And the kingdom and dominion and the greatness of the kingdom under the whole heaven shall be given to the people of the saints of the Most High, whose kingdom is an everlasting kingdom, and *all dominions shall serve and obey him.*

No. 13. RESPONSIVE READING.

Leader.—The Lord reigneth; let the earth rejoice; let the multitude of the isles be glad thereof. Ps. 97:1.

Band.—Therefore glorify ye the Lord, even the name of the Lord God of Israel in the isles of the sea. From the uttermost part of the earth have we heard songs, even glory to the righteous. Isa. 24:15, 16.

L.—This gospel of the kingdom shall be preached in all the world for a witness unto all nations. Matt. 24:14.

Band.—Moreover, thou gavest them kingdoms and nations. Neh. 9:22.

L.—Listen, O isles, unto me; and hearken, ye people, from far. Isa. 49:1.

Band.—Let them give glory unto the Lord, and declare his praise in the islands. Isa. 42:12.

L.—He prophesied that Jesus should die for that nation; and not for that nation only, but also that he should gather together in one the children of God that were scattered abroad. John 11:51, 52.

Band.—He . . . hath made of one blood all nations of men for to dwell on all the face of the earth, and hath determined the times, before appointed, and the bounds of their habitation, that they should seek the Lord. Acts 17:26, 27.

L.—Ask of me, and I shall give thee the heathen for thine inheritance, and the uttermost parts of the earth for thy possession. Ps. 2:8.

Band.—They also that dwell in the uttermost parts are afraid at thy tokens; thou makest the outgoings of the morning and evening to rejoice. Ps. 65:8.

L.—The isles saw it, and feared; the ends of the earth were afraid, drew near and came. Isa. 41:5.

Band.—Many isles were the merchandise of thine

hand; they brought thee for a present horns of ivory and ebony. Ezek. 27 : 15.

L.—Behold, the nations are as a drop of a bucket, and are counted as the small dust of the balance; behold: he taketh up the isles as a very little thing. Isa. 40 : 15.

Band.—He shall not fail nor be discouraged, till he have set judgment in the earth; and the isles shall wait for his law. Isa. 13 : 4.

L.—And the nations of them which are saved shall walk in the light of it; and the kings of the earth do bring their glory and honor into it. Rev. 21 : 24.

Band.—And they sung a new song, saying, Thou art worthy to take the book, and to open the seals thereof: for thou wast slain, and has redeemed us to God by thy blood out of every kindred, and tongue, and people, and nation. Rev. 5 : 9.

No. 14. BIBLE-READING ON SYRIA.

[Prepared for Illustrative Band-meeting; see page 33.]

Leader.—About 1936 B. C. Abraham in Mesopotamia obeys God's call.

1st Member reads Gen. 12 : 1, 5.

L.—God gives him the land.

2d Member, Gen. 13 : 14, 15.

L.—Just before his death, 1451 B. C., Moses gave a summary of its history for three hundred years.

Third Member, Deut. 26 : 5-9.

L.—Four hundred years later, David conquers Syria.

Fourth Member, 2 Sam. 8 : 5, 6.

L.—Five hundred years afterward Ezekiel tells of its riches.

Fifth Member, Ezek. 27 : 16.

L.—When our Saviour was born, five hundred years later, it was a Roman province, including Palestine.
Sixth Member, Luke 2 : 1-3.
L.—Syria hears the gospel.
Seventh Member, Matt. 4 : 24, 25.
L.—Our Saviour visits its northern coasts.
Eighth Member, Mark 7 : 24, 31.
L.—About fourteen years after our Lord's death and resurrection the first Foreign Missionary Society was formed.
Ninth Member, Acts 13 : 1-3.
L.—The next year the anniversary of this society was held.
Tenth Member, Acts 14 : 26, 27.
L.—When a prisoner on his way to Rome, Paul was permitted to visit his friends in Sidon, thus for the last time treading the soil of Syria.
Eleventh Member, Acts 27 : 2, 3, 4.

No. 15. COLLOQUY BETWEEN FAITH AND DOUBT.
By H. M. J.

Doubt.—There is none righteous, no, not one. There is none that understandeth; there is none that seeketh after God. They are all gone out of the way; they are altogether become unprofitable; there is none that doeth good, no, not one.
Faith.—Behold the Lamb of God that taketh away the sin of the world! All we like sheep have gone astray; we have turned every one to his own way, and the Lord hath laid on him the iniquity of us all.
Doubt.—The carnal mind is enmity against God, for it is not subject to the law of God, neither indeed can be.

Faith.—If any man be in Christ Jesus, he is a new creature. Old things are passed away. Not by works of righteousness which we have done, but according to his mercy, he saved us by the washing of regeneration and the renewing of the Holy Ghost.

CHORUS.—Unto Him that loved us and washed us from our sins in his own blood, and hath made us unto our God, kings and priests unto God and his Father, to him be glory and dominion for ever and ever!

Doubt.—They do not return unto the Lord their God, nor seek him for all this. There is no fear of God before their eyes.

Faith.—Jesus said, I came not to call the righteous, but sinners to repentance. I am sought of them which asked not for me. I am found of them that sought me not. God so loved the world that he gave his only-begotten Son. that whosoever believeth in him should not perish, but have everlasting life.

CHORUS.—How beautiful upon the mountains are the feet of him that bringeth good tidings, that publisheth peace, that bringeth good tidings of good, that publisheth salvation, that saith unto Zion, Thy God reigneth!

Faith.—Behold, there shall come from far, and lo, these from the north and from the west, and these from the land of Sinim.

Doubt.—Can the Ethiopian change his skin or the leopard his spots, that they may also do good that are accustomed to do evil?

Faith.—A new heart will I give you, and a new spirit will I put within you, and I will take away the stony heart out of your flesh, and will give you a heart of flesh.

Doubt.—Who hath believed our report, and to whom is the arm of the Lord revealed?

Faith.—He shall not fail nor be discouraged till he hath set judgment in the earth. The isles shall wait for his law. The pleasure of the Lord shall prosper in his hand. He shall see of the travail of his soul, and shall be satisfied.

Chorus.—There was given unto him dominion and glory and a kingdom, that all people, nations and languages should serve him. His dominion is an everlasting dominion which shall not pass away, and his kingdom that which shall not be destroyed.

A Single Voice.—What, then, shall we say to these things? If God be for us, who can be against us? Jesus said repentance and remission of sins should be preached in his name among all nations.

Doubt.—How, then, shall they call on Him in whom they have not believed, and how shall they believe in Him of whom they have not heard, and how shall they hear without a preacher, and how shall they preach except they be sent?

Faith.—Jesus said, As the Father has sent me, even so send I you. Go ye into all the world, and preach the gospel to every creature. Ye shall receive power after that the Holy Ghost is come upon you, and ye shall be witnesses unto me, both in Jerusalem and in all Judæa and in Samaria, and unto the uttermost parts of the earth.

Chorus.—Therefore, seeing we have this ministry, we faint not, for the weapons of our warfare are not carnal, but mighty through God to the pulling down of the strongholds of Satan. Blessed be the Lord God, the God of Israel, who only doeth wondrous things. Blessed be his glorious name for ever, and let the whole earth be filled with his glory. Amen and Amen.

ILLUSTRATIVE BAND-MEETING.

Synopsis of an Illustrative Band-Meeting, given at the Twelfth Annual Meeting of the W. F. M. S.

[The exercises occupied one hour, and were participated in by seventeen young ladies and six children. All the facts used in preparing the papers, etc. were drawn from *The Foreign Missionary, Woman's Work for Woman, Children's Work for Children,* and Dr. H. H. Jessup's books.]

ARRANGED BY MRS. R. H. ALLEN.

Leader read Psalm 67.

All rose and sang, "Praise God from whom," etc., without announcement, and repeated the Lord's Prayer in concert while standing.

Minutes of the last meeting were read.

(Motion to approve made and seconded, and vote taken upon the minutes.

Treasurer's report. (Motion to accept, and vote taken as before.)

Librarian's report. (Vote taken.)

Leader asked, "Is there any unfinished business? Any new business?"

Two verses of a hymn, "Rejoice and be glad," were sung.

Leader announced the subject of the meeting thus: "As our subject is Syria, we will have a Bible-reading that will briefly sketch over two thousand years in its history, remembering that in O.-T. times Syria, Phœnicia and Palestine, or the Land of Canaan, were three distinct provinces. Syria, as then so called, lay east of the Lebanon Mountains, with Damascus as its capital. The country now called Syria includes these three provinces." (See page 28.)

Leader.—"We will now consider ourselves a company of missionaries going to Syria under the guidance of Miss ——, who will show us the way."

A member then showed the route by means of a map of the world, and described some of the sights by the way.

After landing at Beirut the Leader asked: "What missionaries will meet us here?"

Answered by a member.

The Leader said, "We will now hear something of the *Physical Features of Syria.*"

A member, with the aid of a map of Syria, described in about two minutes the chief physical characteristics, also mentioning the varieties of climate, of fruit, etc. The journey was then pursued to the other four stations of our Board in turn, the mode of traveling, the length of time occupied and the character of the country passed through being mentioned. As each station was reached the Leader inquired, "What missionaries are here?" and the answers were given by different members. At Zahleh the question was asked, "Are there any missionary *babies* here?" and answered by a child.

A member read a paper on the *History and Government of Syria*, occupying two minutes.

An Arab boatman's song was sung by a member.

A paper on the *People of Syria*, about two minutes long, was read.

Leader.—"In one evening we cannot visit all of the cities of Syria, but we will hear about three remarkable ones from three of the children."

Three children about eight or ten years of age then successively pointed out Damascus, Tyre and Antioch on the map, and gave a short, simple sketch of each in child-like language.

A paper on the *Work of our Board* in Syria was read, occupying three or four minutes.

One verse of "The whole wide world for Jesus" was sung.

Leader.—"The questions given at our last meeting will now be answered by the members to whom they were assigned."

The Secretary read the questions, as follows:

1. Why is it more difficult to make a convert from Mohammedanism than from any other religion?

2. What remarkable work is being done by the Printing-Press at Beirut?

3. Does Syria sustain important relations to any European country?

4. Are there railroads, telegraph-lines or other "modern improvements" in Syria?

Leader.—"We will now hear any items that have been gathered during the month by the item-gatherers."

One about the "Syrian Boys" (see page 45) was given by a little boy four years old. Others, entitled "Two Girls of Safita" and "The Grand Mosque of Damascus," were given by members.

The Leader then announced the collection, and while it was being taken, a recitation, "Missionary Music," was given by a little boy.

The Leader then opened the Question-Box, and answered the questions she found there.

These were as follows:

1. Do the Mohammedans have Koran societies as we have Bible societies?

2. What does *Ras* Beirut mean?

3. Is it true that a strict Mohammedan will not

have his likeness taken nor have a picture in his house?

A composition written by a little African girl in a mission-school was then read by a member. (See *Foreign Missionary*, May, 1882.)

The Programme Committee announced a programme for the next meeting, recommending that the study of Syria be continued, and assigning to different members the following subjects for papers, etc.: Some account of the life of Mrs. Sarah L. Smith, one of the early missionaries; some information about the *young* ladies now connected with the Syria mission; description of the last commencement in the Sidon School; sketch of the Beirut Seminary and the Protestant College; Bible scenes in Bethlehem and description of modern Bethlehem. *Questions.*—Who translated the Bible into Arabic, and how long did it take? What kind of currency is used in Syria? Where is there a great Mohammedan college containing ten thousand students? The choir to furnish one special piece of music, a story to be read by a member, and items from the item-gatherers as usual. This programme was adopted, and the meeting was closed by singing the "Missionary Hymn," with recitation by a member.

LIST OF SUBJECTS FOR MEETINGS.

SUGGESTIONS FOR STUDY IN YOUNG LADIES' BANDS.

Superstitions of the Heathen.
The Heaven of the Heathen.
Missionary Ships (the first one sent out by the Moravians in 1748).
The birthplace of the A. B. C. F. M. ("Mission Park," Williamstown, Mass.).
How the Heathen Pray.
Condition of Widows in India.
The Caste System.
The Missionary Hymn ("From Greenland's icy mountains"), and how it came to be written.
The First Band of Missionaries who left the U. S. for a Heathen Land.
The Story of the Baptism of over Seventeen Hundred Hawaiian Converts at the same time.
Our Mission-Schools.
Remarkable Answers to Prayer in Missionary Work.
Life of Bishop Patterson.
Life of Harriet Newell.
Lives of the Mrs. Judsons.
Life of Livingstone.
Miss Rankin's Work in Mexico.
Funeral Ceremonies in Heathen Lands.
History of Madagascar.

[The following will show the importance of preserving the back numbers of magazines for reference.]

RELATING TO WOMAN'S WORK.

"The Proportion of Women-Workers to Heathen Women in China," *Woman's Work for Woman*, Feb., '79, p. 40.

"The Woman-Phase in California," Ibid., Nov., '78, p. 306.

"An Incident at Tokio," Ibid., March, '77, p. 7.

"The Work Blessed in India," Ibid., March '77, p. 13.

"A Missionary Society at Woodstock," Ibid., July, '78, p. 191.

"At Chieng-mai, Laos Mission, Siam," Ibid., Nov., '78, p. 309.

"At Soochow, China," Ibid., Sept., '78, p. 256.

"A Christian Woman's Home," Ibid., March, '78, p. 73.

"One of those Helped," Ibid., May, '78, p. 120.

"Miss McBeth among the Nez Percés," Ibid., July, '79, p. 222.

"Miss Hennequin's Letter from Mexico," Ibid., March, '79, p. 81.

"Tours in Persia," Ibid., March, '79, p. 99.

"Among the Moslem Women," Ibid., Dec., '80, p. 407.

"Testimony of the Earl of Shaftesbury about the Needs of Women in India," Ibid., Feb., '80, p. 57.

Additional references may be found in the *Foreign Missionary*, July, '72, p. 53; *Life and Light* for May, '78, p 136; Oct., '79, p. 353; Nov., '79, p. 411.

MEDICAL MISSIONS.

"The Need of Medical Missions," *For. Miss.*, April, '81, p. 481.

"Medical Work in India," *W. W. for W.*, March, '77, p. 1.

"An Appeal," Ibid., July, '81, p. 231.

"Scenes in Africa," *Life of George Paul*, pp. 188 and 190.

"Scenes in Persia," *W. W. for W.*, Jan., '82, p. 14.

"A Medical Missionary in China," Ibid., June, '78, p. 156.

"Dr. Hepburn's Dispensary at Yokohama," *Ch. W. for Ch.*, April, '77, p. 54.

"An Account of the Great Need in Siam" may be found in *Siam, the Land of the White Elephant*, by Geo. H. Bacon; other articles are in *Miss. Herald*, for May, '81, p. 193; *Monthly Record*, for July, '80; *Miss. Her.*, May, '81, p. 192; *W. W. for W.*, March, '81, p. 81; Feb., '81, p. 40, China; and May, '81, p. 149, Siam.

SOME CURIOUS DOINGS,

Recorded in "Children's Work for Children."

"Incense-bearers in Soochow, China," March, '76, p. 42.

"A Chinese Bellringer," June, '79, p. 88.

"Spirit Services in China," Feb., '78, p. 25.

"Pilgrims at Benares, India," April, '76, p. 56.

"Sewing in India," Aug., '76, p. 116.

"A Brahmin Worshiper," Jan., '77, p. 13.

"Trial by Ordeal in India," June, '78, p. 84.

"Caste in India," April, '82, p. 58.

"A Japanese Ride," Sept., '77, p. 132.

"The Shoes of Syrian Boys," Dec., '77, p. 178.

"Calf-Worship among the Druses," Sept., '78, p. 130.

"The Mussulman at Prayer," Dec., '78, p. 184.
"A Mohammedan School," Jan., '77, p. 1.
"The White Ants in Siam," Jan., '77, p. 1.
"An Elephant's Funeral in Siam," March, '78, p. 38.
"Butter-making in Brazil," Aug., '78, p. 122.

ABSURDITIES OF HEATHENISM.

"Adventures of Puss in Heathendom," *Ch. W. for Ch.*, Jan., '81, p. 10.
"Japanese Praying-Machine," Ibid., Sept., '80, p. 138.
"A New God," Ibid., Feb., '81, p. 26.
"An Ancestral Hall in China, Ibid., July, '81, p. 104.
"An Indian Medicine-Man," Ibid., July, '81, p. 108.
"A Chinese Idol," Ibid., April, '79, p. 58.
"Praying in Persia," Ibid., July, '79, p. 110.

MISSIONARY MAP-MAKING.

[The following will give an idea of missionary map-making.]

MISS HARVEY'S BAND.

They were very busy: the map of South America must be ready before the next meeting, and to add to their excitement the meeting was to be public; all the fathers and mothers were coming to learn what was going on in South America.

"It is *big*," said Will, the artist, looking with respect on the country spread out before him, and getting ready to transfer it with all care to his square of muslin.

"Yes, and Brazil is big," said Nellie; "it takes the place in South America that the United States do in North America."

"That proves that *your* item is from Brazil," said Will; and he began to make graceful little lines on the muslin.

"How many people for Brazil? Who knows?"

"Eleven millions," said one; "Twelve millions," said another; "Halfway between," said a third; and Will declared that the "weight of testimony" was for twelve millions; so he set the number down at that.

"Now, go ahead.—What town do you want put down, Nellie Stuart?"

"Rio Janeiro, down there on the bay," said Nellie. "And, Will, you must put a church there, and date it 1862—that's the first Protestant church—and put down two people. That's the number with which they started; make a dash, so ——, and put three hundred after the figure 2. There are *more* than three hundred of them now, but I'll put it at that."

"Done!" said Will, finishing his spire with a flourish. "Go ahead.—Annie Lewis, what do you want?"

"Another church," said Annie, "at San Paulo, and —"

"Hold on! Where's that? Oh, I see: it is not more than half an inch away from Rio Janeiro. What's your date?"

"1865. Six marks for the first members. I don't know how many now, but you may put three or four stars around the spire, for they have sent out as many ministers from that little church."

"I want a hand beckoning from Ubatuba," declared Fanny Shaw; "they want missionaries to come there and teach them. They are begging for them."

"A hand beckoning?" said Will, stopping his pencil in dismay. "I don't believe I can do it, but I'll try; here it goes! It has seven or eight fingers, and looks as though it had the palsy."

"I guess I'll have a head shaking for 'No,'" said Arthur Wilson with a laugh; "for they didn't send them any missionary; they hadn't money enough. Isn't that awful?"

"Put an open Bible for me," said Willie Stearns, "in that same Ubatuba; I want it to stand for an old lady who had never heard of it until she was seventy-five years old. Now she has one of her own, and keeps it 'open' too. I'm going to tell at the meeting how she asked one of the missionaries who visited there this question : 'How is it that you knew the good news so long before you came to tell us?'"

"I don't know how to mark my item, said Carrie Stuart. "It is about a man who carried a Bible to one of those coast-villages; he didn't believe in the Bible, but he took it there, and eight families met together and read it, and were all converted. Then the man was so astonished at the change in them that he began to read the Bible for himself, and he was converted."

"That's queer," said Will. "If I could make a man with his eyes shut holding out a light for others to see by, I would."

This delighted the Band, and they insisted on the young artist attempting just that thing; and although he declared that there ought to be a signboard put beside him, reading, "This is a man," the Band said that *they* all knew what it meant, and Carrie Stuart could explain it to the grown folks at the meeting.

"I don't see why they don't make geography maps more like ours," little Edna said, leaning over and gazing admiringly at Will's efforts; "they would be ever so interesting."

"Lucky they don't!" said the artist wiping his forehead; "there would be no more geographies printed."

How hard they worked over that map, there were so many items of interest, and each one had a scheme of his own which he was determined to carry out! They would not give Will any time to "touch up" his magnificent Amazon River, and as for the Brazilian mountains, he complained that they would be mistaken for brush-heaps, because he had to work so fast.

But you ought to have seen it when it was done, each member of the Band having given an item and had it marked in some way. A curious map it was, certainly; bright-colored paints had been used, and lighted candles stood for Sabbath-schools and day-schools, and open Bibles were numerous, and a cluster of marks, standing for little children, had a chain at their feet all broken to pieces; this to picture the fact that no more children are born *slaves*.

I'll tell you something better than to have seen it let your Band set at once to work and make one like it. It is great fun, besides being very useful.

The Pansy.

ILLUSTRATIONS FOR ITEM-GATHERERS.

SHOWING HOW ITEMS MAY BE GATHERED.

A LONELY MISSIONARY PENNY.

A PENNY, telling its story in the *Juvenile Missionary Magazine*, gives a glimpse of its missionary experience as follows:

"But mine was a new box, and I was the first piece of money to be put into it. There had been an annual missionary meeting that very day, and a little girl had brought the box home with her and placed it on the mantelpiece, and then had put in her first penny. I was that penny, and I do hope you will pity me. *I pity the first penny or the first shilling, or the first of any sort, that is put into a missionary-box.* Just think how dreadfully lonely it is! We do not mind the dark—we are used to it, for we generally live in people's purses and pockets—but we do like being together, having always been accustomed to one another's society. I hope that all who put us into missionary-boxes will remember this: Never put in one of a kind without quickly putting in another, if only for company's sake. If somebody puts in a shilling, never rest till you have got another shilling. If Aunt Mary gives you half a crown, coax Uncle John or Aunt Eliza to give it a companion. And do that for every sixpenny, fourpenny, threepenny and penny piece that you get. See that every fresh arrival gets its fellow, and this will help you wonderfully to fill your box. Noah's ark was soon filled, because there went in two of every sort."

WHAT A LITTLE BOY'S MITE-BOX ACCOMPLISHED.

A LITTLE boy, three years old, sent the contents of a mite-box, eleven dollars, to Rev. Gerald F. Dale of Syria. The results of that very juvenile seed-sowing are as follows: 1. A Bible for the Baalbec Hotel. 2. A large reference Bible for a friendly Greek priest in a neighboring village. 3. A reference Bible for an influential Greek inquirer. 4. The traveling expenses of a little orphan girl on muleback from her mountain-home to the Sidon Seminary. 5. A reference Bible for a fatherless girl in one of the schools. 6. A pocket Testament for a watchman in a vineyard who has leisure to read. 7. A pocket Testament for a man whose fellow-villagers are so bigoted that no direct mission-work can be done among them. 8. A family Bible for a man of leading influence in another village. 9. A hymn-book for a Christian girl living in Damascus. 10. A reference Bible for a man who had voluntarily aided in the distribution of Testaments. 11. A Bible for the use of a school and prayer-meeting. 12. Four Testaments for poor children who are unable to purchase. 13. A pocket Testament for a man whose business keeps him constantly in the saddle. 14. Several copies of sermons for general circulation.

SYRIAN BOYS.

Recitation for a very Small Boy.

I KNOW something funny about the Syrian boys. When they go to school they take off their shoes and leave them outside the door, but they keep their caps on. Sometimes there are a hundred shoes all in a big pile; and when school is over the boys all rush out and kick and pull to find their own shoes; and sometimes they scream and fight and throw each other down, and the teacher has to come out with his stick and stop the noise. And in school the boys all sit on the floor and study out loud. They rock themselves back and forth, and try to see which can scream the loudest, for if one of them stops the teacher whacks him with his stick.

THE SHIP AND THE CHILDREN.

THERE was once a great ship, tall and beautiful, just finished and ready to be launched. This ship was to sail away over the blue ocean to carry *bread* to some hungry people who were starving for food. But, alas! the workmen found they could not move her into the water, though they pushed with all their might. So the *men* of the place came down to help, and they all pushed and pushed, and moved the great ship just a little, and then she stopped. Then the *women* came to help, and the men and the women gave a mighty push all together, and the ship moved slowly down to the very edge of the water, and there she stopped and would not go an inch farther. So they did not know what to do, until one wise woman said, "Call the children to help." And so they did, and the girls and boys came gladly running to do their part, for they felt sorry for the poor starving people beyond the ocean. Then the men and the women and the children pushed together with all their might, and behold! the tall, stately ship moved off into the water with her white sails spread, and sailed away over the blue sea to carry the bread of life to the perishing heathen; and the Lord who was the owner of the ship looked on well pleased and said, "Even a child is known by his doings, whether his work be pure and whether it be right."

BAKING BABIES.

A MISSIONARY in India visited a house one day where there was a new-born baby, which was about the color of a pink sea-shell. "How pretty!" said the visitor to the mother. "Oh," was the reply, "she'll be black, like the rest of us, after I have put her out in the sun for a few days." And sure enough, when the next call was made the poor baby was found baking in the hot Indian sun, stretched on a bit of board, with only a piece of cotton cloth under its head for a pillow. Its body had been first smeared with mustard-oil, according to the strange fashion in that land. The mothers are much surprised to learn that American children are not treated in the same way.

A LITTLE MISSIONARY.

THERE was a little shepherd-boy in a village east of Sidon who learned the gospel in his village. When he went out with his flock to the mountains he preached to the shepherds and goatherds, and begged them to obey the gospel, to give up lying and swearing, and to love the Saviour. One day he came down to his teacher in the village and said, "*Yu Sidi*, these shepherds won't hear the gospel. But *one* of them will. I *fastened to him* and would not give him up, and now he likes to hear."

DIALOGUES AND EXERCISES.

ON INDIA.

[THIS exercise was given by a Band which comprises the whole Sunday-school, and was so constructed that all members of the school had some share in it. The questions were given out at one meeting, to be answered at the next, each class having a question which they, rising, answered in concert. Care was taken that the answers should be as brief and comprehensive as possible. The president of the Band, who is Superintendent of the school, conducted the exercise. The relative position of this country and India was shown on a globe, and upon large maps journeys were traced and all places mentioned pointed out.]

1. In which of the grand divisions of the world is India?
2. How would you reach India going east?
3. How would you reach it going west?
4. How is it bounded?
5. How large is it, compared with the United States?
6. What high mountain north of India? What is its height, and how does it compare with other mountains of the world?
7. What are the principal rivers of India?
8. Which is the Hindoos' sacred river?

[After this question was answered, a boy repeated a paragraph taken from Miss Brittan's *Talks about India*, p. 205, concerning the Ganges.]

9. What are some of the chief cities of India?
10. Which city do the Hindoos consider peculiarly sacred?

[Here a little girl gave a short account, taken from Dr. Prime's *Around the World*, p. 258, of the superstitious reverence the Hindoos have for Benares. Another little girl recited Mrs. Tilden's hymn,

> "Behold the nations kneeling
> 'Neath far-off Eastern skies!" etc.

Then the whole congregation joined in singing the first and third verses of "From Greenland's icy mountains."]

11. What is the climate of India?
12. What are some of the productions?
13. What is the population?

[Several little boys gave short items concerning the people of India, their dress, mode of living, etc.]

14. How many languages are spoken in India?
15. What are the classic languages—the ones in which the sacred books are written?
16. How long ago is it supposed the oldest of these books were written?
17. When did India first appear in authentic history?
18. What European power controls India, and how did it obtain that control?

[This was answered by the Assistant Superintendent, and took the form of a short address. It having been ascertained that he would have something to say about the rise and fall of dynasties and kingdoms, he was asked to close his remarks in such a way as to render appropriate the verse,

> "Crowns and thrones may perish,
> Kingdoms rise and wane," etc.,
> "*Onward, Christian Soldiers,*" verse 3,

which was sung by all present.]

19. What is caste?
20. What are the principal religions of India, and their characteristics?
21. How many gods have the Hindoos?

22. What is the name of their chief idol, and what does it mean?

23. What are some of the things Hindoos do to gain the favor of their gods?

[A very little girl repeated,

"Behold the heathen waits to know
The joy the gospel will bestow,
The exiled captive to receive
The freedom Jesus has to give."

A young lady sang,

"Tell me the story of Jesus,
Write on my heart every word."

Quiver, p. 52.]

24. What Mission Boards are represented in India?

25. What are the names of some of the first American missionaries who went to India?

26. Where are the mission-stations of our Presbyterian Church?

27. In what city is the school to which *this* Band annually contributes?

[This was answered by the smallest class in school; one of the little girls of the class, coming forward, pointed to the place on the map, and then gave a short description of it. A young lady read part of a letter from the teacher of the school, giving an encouraging account of the work there. Then all joined in singing,

"Hear the news, glad news of Jesus:
He is coming now this way."

Crowning Triumph, p. 63.]

28. How do Missionaries work among the people of India, and what progress has been made?

[This was answered by the pastor in a little speech, summing up the whole exercise.]

SYRIA.

A Dialogue for Five Little Girls.

Emma.—I nearly always like to study and hear about the different countries that we have every month in our Mission-Band, but I must say I think Syria is so dull; I do not know anything about it.

Beatrice.—Perhaps that is just the reason you find it dull. Why, it is the very country where Jesus was born and lived, to which the wise men came from the East. I have been reading about it, and I think it just wonderful.

Em.—Do you? Tell us about it, please. I do not know even how far it is, nor how one would get there.

Ada.—Is it a very large country? And how are the people different from us?

Bea.—Well, girls, do not ask so many questions at once, and I will try to tell you the little I know. Syria is about as large as Ohio, and it is nearly a third of the distance around the world from Cincinnati to Jerusalem.

Lulu.—I suppose if you wanted to go there you would have to cross the ocean to Europe or France, take steamer there, and go to Alexandria in Egypt, and from there go by steamer again to Syria; at least that would be one way.

Bea.—Just think, girls! It is the oldest country in the world, and you all know that Damascus is the oldest city. Why, it is four thousand years old, and some say that a grandson of Noah founded it!

Lu.—Oh, I know about Damascus. There is where Naaman the leper lived, that great captain whose wife had a little Jewish captive maiden to wait on her, and she told him to go to Elisha, a prophet in her own country, and he would tell him how to be cured. He went, and Elisha told him to wash in the river Jordan seven times and he would be well. At first, you know, he would not, because he said the rivers of Damascus were so much better, but afterward he went and got perfectly cured.

Ada.—Why, is Damascus in Syria?

Bea.—Yes indeed, and Tyre and Sidon, Antioch. Beirut, and others that I do not know so much about.

Gertrude.—Was it not at Damascus that Paul was let down in a basket from a window by night when he wanted to escape from the Jews?

Bea.—Yes. Many of the houses are made of mud baked hard and white in the sun, and some of them are built on the wall that surrounds the city; so, you see, they could easily have let him down from one of these.

Lu.—And the street called Straight is still there, although most of the streets are crooked, narrow and dirty. The shops are called *bazaars*, and are so small that the shopkeepers put the articles they wish to sell outside on the street, and then sit down among them and wait for buyers.

Ada.—It must be funny to see the second stories of the houses built partly over the streets; they must seem dark and crowded.

Em.—But they have such beautiful gardens and some fine stone buildings. Does it not seem dreadful that the Mohammedans should own this beautiful city, and nearly all the people be followers of the prophet Mohammed?

Bea.—But the missionaries have schools there, and the parents let their children come to learn English and to sew and embroider. A gentleman said that as he was walking along the street one day he heard a child's voice singing, "Come to Jesus;" he stopped in astonishment, and he said he could not keep the tears of pleasure back to hear that sung there. So, you see, they learn in the school our own Sunday-school hymns.

Ger.—And just think, girls, the very first time that the name "Christian" was given was at Antioch! Don't you remember it says in Acts, "And the disciples were first called Christians at Antioch"? Don't it seem strange when there are so few Christians there now?

Lu.—I think Tyre is so wonderful. You know it is on the sea-coast, and part of it was built on an island and part on the land. It was a great, wicked city—so rich that it sent its ships all over the then known world, and people came from a great distance to buy many things there. Why, everybody knew about Tyre as we know about London or New York.

Em.—And yet in Ezekiel it says it should be destroyed, and should never be any more.

Ada.—And has it come true? Is there no city there now?

Bea.—No, only a small place; its fishermen have only a few poor boats, and in the places where stood its beautiful palaces they say it is as bare as the top of a rock, and the fishermen spread their nets to dry on what is left of its great walls.

Ada.—And it says, too, in Ezekiel, something about " scraping her dust from her, and making her like the top of a rock;" and it says, " It shall be a place for the spreading of nets in the midst of the sea."

Em.—I remember, girls, that Hiram, king of Tyre, sold cedars of Lebanon to King David and King Solomon to use in building the temple.

Ger.—Do you know, girls, that now they look upon the mountains of Lebanon as holy, and there are two hundred monasteries built on them, where ten thousand priests live?

Em.—What I want to know is, do the people who live there now know about the disciples and the wonderful things that happened there? and do they love and read the Bible?

Bea.—Not many of them do, and *they* have been taught by the missionaries. The sultan of Turkey rules Syria now, and the greater part of the people are Mohammedans, who study and believe only the Koran; they call us infidels, and are very bitter against us, but not so bad as they used to be.

Ada.—And then in this very land, where Jesus was born, lived and was crucified, perhaps they will learn to love him.

Lu.—Well, let us all pray for the missionaries there, and help them in every way we can.

Em.—Do you suppose that the little girls and boys in Bethlehem know that Jesus was born there?

Ger.—Not many of them do, but three years ago some ladies went and started a school there, and they now have from twenty to thirty little girls whom they teach about Jesus and his wonderful birth. Don't you think it must be beautiful to see the very places?

Lu.—Yes, indeed I do, and I read that they have not got a very good place for the school now, so they are going to build a new one near the fields where the shepherds watched their flocks that Christmas Night when the angel came and told them that Jesus was born.

Bea.—Well, now, Emma, don't you feel more interest in Syria, and would you not like to help those people to know more about Jesus?

Em.—Yes, indeed I do; and I mean to find out a great deal more about it, and do all one little girl can to bring about the glorious time when all shall know Jesus, from the least to the greatest.

COLLECTING FOR MISSIONS.

A Dialogue.

[Several young ladies seated around the table, representing a women's missionary meeting; three young girls acting as solicitors for the mission cause; one very small child; Mrs. A., President; Mrs. D., Treasurer.]

Mrs. A.—The only business before the meeting is the report of our solicitors.

Mrs. B.—I think it is quite time we should transfer some of our mission-work to younger hands.

Mrs. E.—You do not tire of mission-work?

Mrs. B.—Oh no, indeed, but we have to admit that we are growing older every day, and it is well for us to train our young friends, so that they may take our places by and by.

Mrs. A.—While we are waiting, let us see if little Lizzie has her recitation nicely learned for the next mission concert.

Mrs. D.—Put her up in a chair, she is such a little midge.

Mrs. A. (lifting Lizzie into a chair).—Now, Lizzie dear, speak slow and clear, so all can hear.

Lizzie.—I am a very little thing, as you can plainly see;
  But then I know who came to bring God's gift of love to me.

  When I am well I know who makes my life so fair and bright;
  When I am sick I know who takes care of me day and night.

And when I die I know whose hand will lead my soul away
Through death's dark valley to the land where it is always
    day.

Just such little girls as I live over the ocean wave:
They do not know who came to die a sinful world to save.

Poor little heathen!—Friends, I pray that you will
    quickly go,
Or send somebody, right away, to tell them—*all I know.*

Mrs. A. (*taking Lizzie down*).—That's Lizzie's mission-offering. I think if Jesus were here he would say, "She hath done what she could."

Mrs. C.—Here come our young solicitors, Alice, Carrie and Susie. (*They enter.*)

The Ladies.—Good-evening, girls.

Girls.—Good-evening, ladies.

Mrs. B.—I hope you bring us heaps of money, and that you have enjoyed making the calls.

Alice.—We really have enjoyed them, though in various ways. Shall we tell our experience?

Mrs. A.—Yes, if you please.

Carrie.—First, we called on Mrs. Brisk. That visit was finished in a hurry, I assure you. "Missionary-offering?" said she. "Oh, yes indeed! walk right in. It's all counted out. I thought you'd be along soon. Here it is; I can't say I wish it was more, because it's just according to my means, and the Lord has the regulating of them. I won't ask you to sit down, for I suppose you've ever so many places to go to; besides, I'm busy as a bee myself." So off she flew, and we walked off, having obtained that dollar in less time than I have taken to tell of it.

Mrs. M.—Where next?

Susie.—We went in succession to Mrs. Kindly's, Mrs.

Allright's and Mrs. Ready's. They each had a pleasant word for us, and cheerfully gave their contributions.

Carrie.—Mrs. Kindly said it was very good in us to go around in this way and save people the trouble of sending in their money. Here are their gifts—three, five and two dollars. Now, Alice, you tell the next story. (*Giving money to Mrs. D.*)

Alice.—Are we to relate all our experience, good or bad?

Mrs. B.—We'd like to know it all.

Alice.—Well, then, our next visit was to Mrs. Splendid. "*Mission*-money?" said she. "*What* mission?" "For our mission-school," we told her. "*What* mission-school?" So I told her about our mission-school in India that we have supported so many years—of the wonderful good it has accomplished, and of the work it is now doing, and how glad we were to be the means of carrying it on. I thought I was really making such a moving speech.

Carrie.—It proved so; Mrs. Splendid very stiffly replied, "I have many ways for my money, young ladies; I have nothing for you to-day." And she moved in and we moved out. Just think of it! Such lots of money as Mrs. Splendid has! and how she dresses!

Mrs. C.—Hush! hush! my dear. Here, girls, is a lesson for you: When you meet with such rebuffs, take them in a gentle spirit. Don't allow yourself to judge hastily, but try to feel kindly toward those who seem selfish and ungenerous, and then dismiss them utterly from your thoughts as quickly as Mrs. Splendid sent you from her door.

Susie.—Can't we call her "Mrs. *Shabby*," just among ourselves?

Mrs. A.—" Not a bit of it," as you girls say. Say nothing at all about her.

Alice.—Then we went to see lame Jennie. We didn't think she ought to give anything, she is so poor; but Susie said we would go in and tell her what we were doing.

Mrs. E.—Poor, patient little sufferer! what had she to say?

Carrie.—She clapped her little thin hands and said she was so glad we had come. She had been thinking so much, since she cannot go to church and Sunday-school any more, of the heathen children who never had any church or Sunday-school, and who never heard the " Suffer little children " that Jesus said; and of the poor little lame heathen sufferers who never heard of the land where " the inhabitants shall not say, ' I am sick.' "

Mrs. B.—But of course you did not ask her to give you anything?

Susie.—"Ask her?" We hadn't the chance. She said at once, " You must have my mission-offering, only you will need to wait while I go to the bank for it."

Mrs. C.—" Go to the bank," when she cannot walk a step?

Alice.—Yes, she took her little tin "savings bank," and made believe knock at the door. "Any money for me to-day?" she said.—" How much do you want?" she made believe come in a gruff voice from within.— " Fifty cents," said she.—" What do you want it for?" in the same deep voice.—" For my missionary-offering," said Jennie.—" Yes, yes! here it is; come down the chimney and get it." (You know we have to turn the pennies out at the chimney-top.) So she counted them out and gave them to us.

Carrie.—I asked if she wouldn't need it for something. She said No; it was given her for candy-money, but if she liked missionary-candy better than molasses-candy, she thought she should have her choice.

Mrs. D.—We don't need to tell you to learn a lesson from her sweet, self-denying spirit.

Susie.—No, I think not. We were intending to buy each a new ribbon; we had been choosing between blue and pink. As we came out, Alice said, "Girls, how would missionary-ribbon suit you?" We took the hint, and all decided to have just that color. (*Handing the price of the ribbon to Mrs. D.*)

Alice.—As we are indebted to Jennie for the example, we think the money should be credited to her.

Mrs. A.—That is just right. She will be so happy to know that her simple example influenced you in so good a way.

Mrs. B.—Did you call on Mrs. Dillydally?

Carrie.—Yes, ma'am. She said, "Well, she'd see; she didn't know. How much'd the deacon's wife give? How much'd the pastor's wife give? For her part, seemed to her there was always something coming—missions or *something*. We might call again; she'd see."

Mrs. C.—And Mrs. Sharp?

Susie.—Oh yes! She said, "Mr. Sharp gave enough, *goodness* knows! *She* couldn't be bothered;" and she said her good-morning to us as quickly as Mrs. Brisk, but oh, in such a different tone!

Mrs. D.—Here are five dollars more than your list of names accounts for. How is that?

Alice.—I'll tell you; it was so funny! We saw Mr. Cross coming down the street. You know he is rich as rich can be, but he doesn't believe in missions nor Sunday-schools, nor anything of the kind. Carrie said, "Let's storm the enemy's fortress and see what we can get."

Carrie.—So we bade him good-morning, told him all about our mission-school, and politely asked him for a contribution.

Mrs. A.—What did he say?

Carrie.—He lifted both hands, and rolled up his eyes, and said,

> "Hark! hark! hark! hear the dogs bark!
> The *beggars* are coming to town!"

That roused me. I told him we were *not* "beggars;" that we were very young, but we were learning to work in the mission cause because it was a good cause, and we meant to do all we could for the heathen people who are living in sin and ignorance, and we would thank him never to call us beggars again.

Mrs. E.—I hope you didn't make him angry.

Alice.—I guess not. He looked steadily at Carrie, as though he was thinking of what she had said. Then the queer man said, "Hold out your hands." We did so, and he dropped a penny into each of them, saying, "*That's* for your missions." Then he raised his hat and made a low bow to Carrie, and putting five dollars in her hand, said, "Respected madam, *that* is for your *preach*."

Mrs. C.—Well done, Carrie! I never before knew a mission "preach" reach that man's purse. I hope the effect may be lasting.

Mrs. B.—You had Mrs. Flutter's name; what did she say?

Susie.—She said, "Deary-me, no! She just couldn't. Everything was so high! Bad as war-times! Elizabeth Eliza was taking music-lessons, and, deary-me it costs so! And Elizabeth Eliza must have a new summer silk, and 'Charity begins at home,' and, deary-me, she just *couldn't*." So she didn't.

Alice.—Oh, but the last place was so different! Dear Grandmother Elder gave her dollar with her poor, trembling fingers, and then she talked to us so sweetly!

Carrie.—Yes; she told us how glad she was that we were beginning so young to work in the dear Lord's vineyard. Then she showed us a little ivory box on her shelf, in which she had kept her mission-money for forty years.

Susie.—And she said, "Next year, my dears, when you come, I don't think I shall be here. I think I shall be in the beautiful city whose gates are of pearl. But my offering I shall leave in the little box, and you may open it and take it." Then she blessed us, and we came away.

Mrs. D.—Young ladies, we are highly gratified with your report. You have not only brought us a good sum of money, but your experience has been both useful to yourselves and interesting to us.

Mrs. A.—We will now close our meeting by singing, "The whole wide world for Jesus."—*Heathen Woman's Friend.*

THE CHURCH MILITANT.

By Miss Adelia Hamilton.

Leader.—In what character are we now assembled?

School.—As soldiers anxious to invade the country of our enemy.

L.—Against whom do we wage warfare?

S.—Against the prince of this world.

L.—For whom do we fight?

S.—For Jesus Christ, the Captain of our salvation.

L.—How must we be equipped?

S.—We must take unto ourselves the whole armor of God, that we may be able to withstand in the evil day, and having done all, to stand.

School sing:
"Soldiers of Christ, arise,
 And put your armor on,
Strong in the strength which God supplies
 Through his eternal Son;
Strong in the Lord of hosts,
 And in his mighty power,
Who in the strength of Jesus trusts
 Is more than conqueror."

L.—How long shall the contest continue?

S.—Till every inch of the enemy's country is ours and the banner of Immanuel floats over the world.

L.—How do we know that victory is certain?

S.—Because the Father has promised the Son the heathen for an inheritance, and the uttermost parts of the earth for a possession, that at the name of Jesus every knee shall bow, and every tongue confess that Jesus Christ is Lord, to the glory of God the Father.

School sing:
"Jesus shall reign where'er the sun
 Does his successive journeys run;
 His kingdom spread from shore to shore,
 Till moons shall wax and wane no more.

"To him shall endless prayer be made,
 And endless praises crown his head;
 His name like sweet perfume shall rise
 With every morning sacrifice."

L.—Where has our great enemy his strongholds?

S.—Wherever human footsteps tread the soil—in

Greenland or in Lapland, in the cold, bleak wastes of Siberia and the hot, barren desert of Sahara, as well as in some of the fairest portions of God's heritage, where the tall palm tree waves its graceful branches and tropical fruits and flowers lade the air with their perfume, where birds in endless variety flit about on wings of rainbow hue, and Nature keeps perpetual holiday.

School sing:

> "From Greenland's icy mountains,
> From India's coral strand;
> Where Afric's sunny fountains
> Roll down their golden sand;
> From many an ancient river,
> From many a palmy plain,—
> They call us to deliver
> Their land from error's chain."

L.— If we cannot personally join in the combat on a foreign soil, how can we help on the invasion?

*S.—*By securing recruits, by contributing supplies, and by following the invading army with our prayers.

*L.—*Mention some who thus aid in conquering this world for Christ.

*S.—*The scholar who denies himself a pleasure that he may place the price in the Lord's treasury; the poor widow who, having not even the two mites to bestow, gives her prayers; and all who hush nature's repinings that they may send their bravest and best to the battle.

School sing:

> "Come, let us with a grateful heart
> In this great labor share a part;
> Our prayers and offerings gladly bring
> To aid the triumphs of our King."

L.—By what name do we call those who are sent out to this work?

S.—Missionaries.

L.—Who were the first Christian missionaries?

S.—The apostles.

L.—When and where was the first great battle fought?

S.—In Jerusalem, on the day of Pentecost.

L.—With what result?

S.—A glorious victory.

L.—How many were ransomed from the enemy?

S.—About three thousand, who immediately joined the ranks in the army of our Immanuel.

L.—What strong points are our forces attacking?

S.—Satan's, wherever they are.

L.—Are we gaining ground?

S.—Thank God, we are! There have been years of patient waiting, when our missionaries have gone forth weeping, bearing precious seed to sow beside all waters. They now begin to come again with rejoicing, bringing their sheaves with them.

School sing:

"Sow in the morn thy seed;
　At eve hold not thy hand;
To doubt and fear give thou no heed:
　Broadcast it o'er the land.

"Thou canst not toil in vain;
　Cold, heat and moist and dry
Shall foster and mature the grain
　For garners in the sky."

L.—Suppose it might be given you to-night to take a peep in foreign lands; tell me some of the scenes you would select.

Voice 1.—I would ask to see a home where the

mother who once threw her babes into the Ganges now rocks them to sleep with a cradle-song about Jesus.

Voice 2.—I would choose a missionary school where heathen boys and girls, gathering around the Christian teacher, learn to read the Bible each in his own strange tongue.

Voice 3.—I would like to watch the bonfires made of their burning idols.

Voice 4.—I would ask to see their kings and queens humbly kneeling for Christian baptism.

Voice 5.—And I would beg to look forward through the years and see the last sinner as he yields to Jesus and tremblingly prays for pardon, while friends and neighbors exultingly cry, "The dead is alive, the lost is found!" The kingdoms of this world have become the kingdoms of our Lord and his Christ.

School sing:

"Then shall the voice of singing
    Flow joyfully along;
Then hill and valley, ringing
    With one triumphant song,
Proclaim the contest ended,
    And He who once was slain
Again to earth descended
    In righteousness to reign.

"Then from the craggy mountains
    The sacred shout shall fly,
And shady vales and fountains
    Shall echo the reply.
High tower and lowly-dwelling
    Shall send the chorus round,
All hallelujahs swelling,
    In one eternal sound."

[The above exercise is published by Garrigues Brothers, Philadelphia. in tract form, and is inserted here by their permission.]

WORK FOR THE LITTLE ONES.

By Marion West.

1st Scholar. We are but little children weak,
    Nor born in high estate;
What can we *do* for Jesus' sake,
    Who is so high, so good, so great?

We know the holy innocents
    Laid down for him their infant life,
And martyrs brave and patient saints
    Have stood for him in fire and strife.

We wear the cross they wore of old,
    Our lips have learned like vows to make:
We need not die; we cannot fight;
    What *may* we do for Jesus' sake?

Class in concert. Jesus said, Suffer the little children to come unto me, and forbid them not; for of such is the kingdom of God. Mark 10 : 14.

2d Sch. Oh, day by day each Christian child
    Has much to do without, within—
A death to die for Jesus' sake,
    A weary war to wage with sin.

3d Sch. When deep within our swelling breasts
    The thoughts of pride and anger rise,
When bitter words are on our tongues
    And tears of passion in our eyes,

Then we may stay the angry blow,
    Then we may check the hasty word,
Give gentle answers back again,
    And fight a battle for the Lord.

4th Sch. With smiles of peace and looks of love
    Light in our dwellings we may make,
Bid kind good-humor brighten them;
    And do all these for Jesus' sake.

5th Sch.   There's not a child so small and weak
        But has its little cross to take,
    Its little work of love and praise,
        That may be done for Jesus' sake.

In concert.   Whether therefore ye eat or drink, or whatsoever
    ye do, do *all* to the glory of God. 1 Cor. 10 : 31.

For Four very Little Ones.

1st.   God make my life a little light
        Within the world to glow—
    A little flame that burneth bright
        Wherever I may go.

2d.   God make *my* life a little flower
        That giveth joy to all,
    Content to bloom in native bower,
        Although its place is small.

3d.   God make *my* life a little song,
        That comforteth the sad,
    That helpeth others to be strong,
        And makes the singer glad.

4th.   God make *my* life a little hymn
        Of tenderness and praise,
    Of faith that never waxeth dim
        In all his wondrous ways.

In concert.   Let us love one another, for love is of God.
    1 John 4 : 7.

(Let the following be spoken by seven little girls, and some one in an adjoining room or in the gallery echo the last two words of each stanza.)

1st   If you've any task to do,
        Let me whisper, friend, to you,
                Do it!   (*Echo*, Do it.)

2d.   If you've anything to say,
        True and needed, yea or nay,
            Say it! (*Echo.*)

3d.   If you've anything to love
        As a blessing from above,
            Love it! (*Echo.*)

4th.   If you've anything to give,
        That another's joy may live,
            Give it! (*Echo.*)

5th.   If you know what torch to light,
        Guiding others through the night,
            Light it! (*Echo.*)

6th.   If you've any debt to pay,
        Rest you neither night nor day,
            Pay it! (*Echo.*)

7th.   If you've any grief to meet,
        At the loving Father's feet
            Meet it! (*Echo.*)

In concert. If ye know these things, happy are ye if ye do them. John 13 : 17.

One of the class. How many deeds of kindness
      A little child may do,
   Although it has so little strength,
      And little wisdom too!
   It wants a loving spirit
      Much *more* than *strength* to prove
   How many things a child may do
      For others by its love.

In concert. Even a child is known by its doings, whether his work be pure, and whether it be right. Prov. 20 : 11.

[The above exercise is published by Garrigues Brothers, Philadelphia, in tract form, and is inserted here by their permission.]

DIALOGUES AND EXERCISES.

ZION'S WATCHMAN.

By Miss Adelia Hamilton.

Class.   O Zion's watchman, is there aught
    Of good to hear or tell?
How fares it with our darkened world?
    Hath evil loosed its spell?
Do the dark places of the earth
    Obey, as well as hear?
Heavy the time, we've waited long;
    Oh for some words of cheer!

Watchman.   The morning light is breaking,
    The darkness disappears;
The sons of earth are waking
    To penitential tears.
Each breeze that sweeps the ocean
    Brings tidings from afar
Of nations in commotion,
    Prepared for Zion's war.

Class.   They say the beauteous rose still climbs
    On fair Damascus' wall,
With breath as sweet as when its cheek
    Flushed at the flight of Paul.
But, ah! in that historic clime
    The Rose of Sharon fair
Anew we plant, with pain and toil;
    How are our laborers there?

Watchman.   Rich dews of grace come o'er us
    In many a gentle shower,
And brighter scenes before us
    Are opening every hour.
Each cry to heaven going
    Abundant answer brings,
And heavenly gales are blowing,
    With peace upon their wings.

Class.   Brahma and Buddha! Will their rule
        Soon pass and cease to be?
    And trusts the learned Brahmin less
        His false philosophy?
    And strange old China—simple, wise—
        To pray does she begin?
    God help our brethren who assail
        Those ancient seats of sin!

Watchman.   See heathen nations bending
        Before the God of love,
    And thousand hearts ascending
        In gratitude and love,
    While sinners, now confessing,
        The gospel call obey,
    And seek a Saviour's blessing,
        A nation in a day.

Class.   Where on Moriah curling rose
        The smoke of sacrifice,
    The harsh-voiced Moslem's call to prayer
        Pierces the weary skies.
    Olivet darkens at the sound,
        And Kedron hastes away;
    Over these hallowed scenes how long
        Must Islam's sword bear sway?

Watchman.   Blest river of salvation,
        Pursue thine onward way;
    Flow thou to every nation,
        Nor in thy richness stay—
    Stay not, till all the lowly
        Triumphant reach their home;
    Stay not, till all the holy
        Proclaim, "The Lord is come."

[The above exercise is published by Garrigues Brothers, Philadelphia, in tract form, and is inserted here by their permission.]

HOW THE FLOWERS WENT TO SCHOOL.

A CONCERT EXERCISE.

By Mrs. R. M. Tuttle.

[PERSONS: A Leader who recites, one as "the Lily," two as "Roses," others as "Leaves," others as "Grasses," and the Class.]

Leader recites.—One day all the flowers went to school in a great garden. They chose one from their own number to be the teacher. It was midsummer, and the one chosen was the field lily. They stood in their places in rows, the tall ones against the wall and the little ones close about the feet of the teacher. She was tall and arrayed in raiment of scarlet and gold, a far-off cousin of the royal tribe of whom the Lord of the whole earth said—

Class (bowing toward the Lily).—" Consider the lilies of the field, how they grow; they toil not, neither do they spin: and yet I say unto you, That even Solomon in all his glory was not arrayed like one of these."

The Lily (taking her place).—The life given us is the life of the grass of the field, " which to-day is and to-morrow is cast into the oven," as it is written—

Class.—" In the morning it flourisheth and groweth up; in the evening it is cut down and withereth."

The Lily.—In the great plan of creation our life, though brief and little, has a place and a purpose—

Class.—"All thy works shall praise thee, O Lord!"—

The Lily.—" To comfort man, to whisper hope
 Whene'er his faith grows dim;
For whoso careth for the flowers
 Will much more care for him."

Class.—" Blessed are they that do his commandments."

The Lily.—Into our life of blossoming are pressed

hours of sunshine, nights of dew, days of shade and showers of rain. The law for all things created is the same: "Give as ye have received," as it is written—

Class.—Freely ye have received—freely give.

The Lily.—We have a part in making the summer beautiful and sweet over the great, wide earth. We are to give of the riches of our brightness and fragrance; give

> As the sun hath shined on us,
> As the rain hath rained on us,
> As the dew hath freshened us,
> As the shade hath shadowed us.

We are to give of such as we have, as it is written—

Class.—"Give . . . of such things as ye have."

Leader recites.—Then began such a buzzing as bees make when the orchards are in full blossom, the green leaves whispered so loud (here the children give the Kindergarten hum of bees, ending at a sign from the Leader in sudden silence), saying—

The Leaves.—What can we do to make the summer-time over the great, wide earth more lovely and sweet?

The Lily.—Grow in your places and make shadow—

The Grasses (bowing to the Leaves).—"For the sun is no sooner risen with a burning heat but it withereth the grass, and the flower thereof falleth and the grace of the fashion of it perisheth." As a well and a palm in the desert, so is your shadow to us. Oh grow and make shade.

Leader recites.—The leaves shook hands each with its neighbor, being in the right way (here each child quickly shakes hands with the next), and went on, just making shadow, weaving a veil to hide the brightness of the face of summer, while the grasses, low at the feet of the lily, murmured—

The Grasses.—Oh, what can we do to make the summer-time over the great, wide earth sweeter for our being here?

The Lily.—Though least of all of us, your work is greatest. Ye are first in spring-time and the last in autumn, weaving for the brown clods of earth a velvet cover whose softness, color and fragrance no art can match.

The Grasses.—Oh, but it's such a little thing, just to be grasses, to be trodden on, and only to grow greenness!

The Lily.—Without grass the herds of cattle would perish that add to the life and comfort of the children of men, the roots of many herbs would die, and there would be no pleasant fields where the strawberries could hide away their ripeness.

Leader recites.—The grasses being comforted, they just went on weaving their matchless mat for the feet of Summer as she went her way over the great, wide earth.

And here two rose trees thrilled from bud to blossom. Throwing off their mantles of green, the one blushed pink and the other blanched white. But they lifted up their voices as one:

The Roses.—Oh, what can we do to make the summer-time sweeter over the great, wide earth?

The Lily.—Just blossom where you are; open your hearts and give to the sun and wind the rose-smells treasured there; and the summer-time over the great, wide earth will be the sweeter for your blossoming.

The Roses.—But our hearts will break when we open wide our blossoms and give to the sun and wind the riches of the rose-smells treasured there.

Class.—"Freely ye have received—freely give." "There is that scattereth and yet increaseth."

Leader recites.—As the roses in a devotion of blossoming poured out their treasures of sweetness, a hand reached into the garden and gathered with a sharp-cutting steel a bunch of the most perfect rose-blooms. Every rose tree, standing in its place in the garden, shook with trembling as the roses were severed from the boughs where they grew to give joy in some place afar off. But the whole garden was filled with the rarest smell of roses.

Class.—When Mary anointed the feet of the Lord of the whole earth with the spikenard very precious, the house was filled with the odor of the ointment.

The Lily.—The wounded stem may bleed and the branch may suffer loss, but it is great honor to be chosen. Because ye gave praiseful growth and bloom and sweetness in your places, it is joy to be chosen to go to make other places glad that are far away. It is to be like the Lord of the whole earth, who gave his life for the children of men, and who said—

Class.—"I am the Rose of Sharon and the Lily-of-the-valley."

The Lily.—The sweetness and beauty which become inwrought and broidered into character live for eternity, while the blossom whose seed matures reproduces its like for time only. Choose to be sent on Love's errands. Choose to give your life that you may save it, and become immortal, as it is written—

Class.—"Whosoever shall lose his life for my sake, shall find it."

All recite.—"It is more blessed to give than to receive;" and we choose, if so we may be chosen, to be the "cut flowers" of the garden; to be severed from the stem that holds us to the home-place; to obey the voice of the Lord of the whole earth, who saith, "Go ye into all the world and preach the gospel to every creature." We choose to be sent on his errands into chambers foul with the breath of sickness or dark with the gloom of sorrow; to whisper hope to the hopeless; to cheer the desolate whose lives have lost color by walking too long in the shadow. We choose to give—

> As the sun hath shined on us,
> As the rain hath rained on us,
> As the dew hath freshened us,
> As the shade hath shadowed us—

to make the summer-time over the great, wide earth full of beauty, until every place near by shall be bright and sweet, and every waste and desert place afar off shall rejoice and blossom as the rose.

CHIMES IN MANY TONGUES.

First.—The first purely native Christian pastor in Japan, educated in his own country, is Mura Kami San, who was ordained in November, 1877. He is not an English scholar, but is well educated in Chinese. He is a patient, even-going, able and devoted minister. He first became interested in Christianity by a book on Christian evidences written in Chinese by Dr. Martin. The next impulse was from the organ playing in the chapel and the singing in Chinese of the hymn—

(*Sing.*)   " To-day the Saviour calls
             Ye wanderers home;
        O ye benighted souls,
             Why longer roam?"

Second.—The day is still and calm in the land of Mohammed, and your surprised ear hears a familiar melody that it has heard in many an assembly in your own country, Christian America. It is three hundred Mohammedan girls singing Ray Palmer's precious hymn—

> (*Sing.*) "My faith looks up to thee,
> Thou Lamb of Calvary,
> Saviour divine;
> Now hear me while I pray:
> Take all my guilt away,
> Oh, let me from this day
> Be wholly thine."

Third.—Go with me to South Africa, to the little village of Umzumbi in Natal. Men and women are coming in every direction from their rude huts toward the mission-school building, where the weekly singing is held with pupils and people on the verandah. They were wild Zulus a few months or years ago. They are bright, inquiring musical Zulus now. They patiently drill for an hour in their own language on the songs and hymns the teacher has taught them. "The hour is ended," she says. Then a clamor of voices is heard, begging, "Izama elinye e English nikosazana, please" ("Sing one hymn in English, princess, please"). Given their choice, they fix upon a favorite, and, led by her clear voice, the whole company, old and young, sing in mixed Zulu and English—

> (*Sing.*) "Oh think of a home over there,
> By the side of the river of light,
> Where the saints all immortal and fair
> Are robed in their garments of white.
>
> *Cho.:* "Over there, over there; oh, think of a home over there;
> Over there, over there; oh, think of a home over there."

Fourth.—Would you like to attend a New Year's watch-meeting among the Dakota Indians? They have stores of good things to eat, a cedar tree for gifts and a northern giant, the Indian St. Nicholas, to distribute presents among the children. They join in prayer with Good Thunder and Big Eagle, listen to exhortations from Mr. Appearing-Flute and Wind-Spear, and are stirred up in regard to the missionary contribution by Mr. Black Lightning. They spend a night of joy, of prayer and of good resolutions for the year to come. Then, as it becomes daylight, before the pastors and deacons go round shaking hands with every one, they all join in singing—

(*Sing.*)   "Ho! my comrades, see the signal
              Waving in the sky!
           Reinforcements now appearing,
              Victory is nigh!

Cho.:   "'Hold the fort, for I am coming,'
              Jesus signals still;
           Wave the answer back to heaven,
            'By thy grace we will'"

Fifth.—We are in Oroomiah, Persia. Yonder is the chapel of the girls' boarding-school, where Sunday-school is being held. Let us enter. Be careful not to stumble over these fifty pairs of shoes around the door outside. Within we meet a cordial welcome from the teacher as pilgrims from her own loved America. The owners of the fifty pairs of shoes are all sitting on the floor, singing with earnestness in their native Syriac—

(*Sing.*)   "Come to the Saviour, make no delay:
            Here in his word he's shown us the way;
            Here in our midst he's standing to-day,
              Tenderly saying, 'Come!'

Cho.: " Joyful, joyful will the meeting be,
    When from sin our hearts are pure and free;
    And we shall gather, Saviour, with thee
        In our eternal home."

Sixth.—The good ship Morning Star, bought by the Sunday-schools of America, is, among the many war-ships of Christendom, one of the few dedicated to the spread of the gospel of peace. Captain Bray writes that last summer, while navigating among the wonderful islands and shoals of the Micronesian mission, stopping as nearly as possible at the doors of the missionaries in the various groups to leave them supplies and news, they anchored one evening just off a point in the lagoon, between two parties of natives who had been at war seven months. Lying at anchor, till morning should again make it safe to go on, at intervals through the night they heard the reports and saw the flashes of the opposing guns. Some missionaries were on board the Morning Star—Mr. and Mrs. Haind—going from one station to another, As the rising sun glittered on the waves that wash those islands of the far South Pacific, these two Christians took their Bibles and went on shore. They first found the party opposing the king, and after some talk two of the chiefs came on board the ship with Mrs. Haind. After a little Mr. Haind came with the king and one of his men. Whatever may have been the cause of the war, the Spirit of Christ disposed them to peace. Mr. Haind drew up a treaty of peace in the Gilbert Island language, which they all signed. Then they shook hands with each other, and before they went on shore to disperse their bands Mr. Haind prayed with them, and from the lately hostile hearts there went out over the waters from the little gospel-yacht this song of peace—

(*Sing.*) "Bright in that happy land
Beams every eye;
Kept by a Father's hand,
Love cannot die."

Seventh.—The natural love of music implanted in the Armenians reminds one of the Germans; and gospel-singing is a power in Turkey. Passing the fields and vineyards, one may hear men and women singing—

(*Sing.*) "Just as I am, without one plea,
But that thy blood was shed for me,
And that thou bidst me come to thee,
O Lamb of God, I come!"

Miss West says that at Aintab, Turkey, there is a Sunday-school of twelve hundred grown people and children in regular attendance. One of the indirect results of this school is sometimes seen in the crowded thoroughfares of the city in the shape of a veritable little Arab, all rags and dirt, sitting astride a loaded donkey, and singing in Turkish at the top of his shrill voice—

(*Sing.*) "I want to be an angel."

If we should leave our own church on Sunday morning and attend worship at Bardezag in Turkey, we should find a long, narrow room with one hundred people sitting on the floor, the men on one side, the women on the other, with children scattered between. Dark mud walls and small windows do not add to the cheerfulness of the place; but after an impressive service, conducted by a graduate of the Mission Seminary at Constantinople, the people all join in spirited singing. Is there something familiar in that tune? It is difficult to tell, disguised as it is in "variations" with

Turkish trills and semiquavers. But it is this grand old universal favorite—

(*Sing.*) "Praise God, from whom all blessings flow;
Praise him, all creatures here below;
Praise him above, ye heavenly host,
Praise Father, Son and Holy Ghost."

A COMPANY OF MISSIONARIES.
By Mrs. W. A. Niles.

President.—We present to you to-day a company of missionaries whose history you will find in a book well known to you all. The first character we bring is our common mother, and although you may have some prejudice against her on account of her bad conduct on one occasion, yet you will all acknowledge that she acted the missionary to us in giving us life through our Redeemer. Hear the promise given for her in the beginning.

Band read Gen. 3 : 15.

Vice-President.—The next character we present as a missionary to the world is Abraham, who lived two thousand years after Eve. Hear the promise made to him by One who is ever faithful to fulfill his word.

Band.—Gen. 22 : 18.

Our third missionary comes to us by a name that means *praise*, and surely "praise" has sounded down the ages from the lips of Judah. Hear the promise made to him.

Band.—Gen. 49 : 10.

Pres.—And now comes one with white locks and flowing beard, who was drawn from the water when he was a very little child, and whom God sent when a man to let the Egyptians know that Jehovah reigned in the earth. His name is Moses. Hear him speak.

Band.—Ex. 9 : 29.

And now the sister of Moses sings sweetly to us with the timbrel and with the dance.

Band.—Ex. 15 : 20.

Nor is she the only woman of olden time who tunes her harp for the listening ear of the world in her mission of love and mercy, for hear the noble Deborah saying—

Band.—Judg. 5 : 1-3.

V.-Pres.—And again we listen to a company of ancient women, as, hand in hand, come Hannah, Ruth and Esther speaking thus:

Band.—1 Sam. 2 : 1, 2; Ruth 1 : 16; Esth. 4 : 16.

But who is this that strikes the lyre and tunes the voice in sweetest notes of praise? A crown of gold is on his head and in his hand a shepherd's crook, and he gathers the sheep like a shepherd and carries the lambs in his bosom. At once a king, a father and a shepherd, hear David sing:

Band.—Ps. 24.

Pres.—And now we have another—his skin fair as a lily, his keen, prophetic eye gazing down into futurity. It was he who refused to be fed with the king's dainties, and who, with the four Hebrew children, gave the gospel of the kingdom to the Chaldæan realm. His name is Daniel. Hear him:

Band.—Dan. 2 : 23.

Our characters, thus far, have appeared to us from the far-remote depths of the living past, from the very beginning, and all have spoken of good things yet to come. Four thousand years in the world's history has the index finger pointed *forward,* and now again we hear the sweet voice of a woman singing glad tidings and proclaiming the coming kingdom. **Hear** Elizabeth, the cousin of Mary:

Band.—Luke 1 : 42, 43.

V.-Pres.—And a still sweeter voice answers, and Mary herself says—

Band.—Luke 1 : 38.

And as the little smiling Babe of Bethlehem appears upon the stage of action, the old and the new meet and rejoice as Anna the prophetess enters the temple.

Band.—Luke 2 : 38.

But the Babe grows to manhood, and in all the glory of his perfect nature reveals to the world the fact that his birth was a heavenly one. He was a missionary sent from heaven to us, and the past melts into the present, and the song and the story grow into a tender meaning, and the darkness gives place to light, as the Seed of the woman bruises indeed the serpent's head, while, halo-circled, he stands and cries—

Band.—John 3 : 16; .12 : 32.

Pres.—The present is past once more, and with the index finger pointing backward appears a sturdy, active, vigorous man in the dress of a fisherman. He was in a trance at mid-day, and there the Spirit taught him the blessed lesson, "What God hath cleansed, that call not thou common," and he gives us his commission, thus:

Band.—John 21 : 15, 16.

We have chosen but two more out of the goodly company of the ancients to tell us to-day the story of the Lamb slain from the foundation of the world. The one who now speaks was once a persecutor, hating and destroying all who dared to speak the name of Jesus or show forth his praise. But in a moment he was changed, and the lips which breathed forth hatred and cruelty now tell with wondrous power and sweetness the story of the Redeemer. Paul gives us the words of his Lord to him:

Band.—Acts 22 : 21.

V.-Pres.—The scene closes. An old man comes, his locks whitened with the snows of many winters. He loves and is beloved, and though his head is silvered, yet in his heart there glows the fervor of an immortal youth. Such love can never die. St. John the Divine speaks to us in the book of Revelation:

Band.—Rev. 1 : 3; 22 : 20.

JUVENILE MISSIONARY MEETING.

Arranged by Alice W. Knox.

Motto on the Blackboard:

> GOD HELPING ME, I WILL.

1. Read in concert Ps. 117.
2. Sing, "Praise God, from whom all blessings flow."
3. Read responsively Ps. 2.
4. Prayer.
5. Read the Motto in concert.
6. Some member read the following:

THE MISSIONARY'S MOTTO.

The Rev. Arthur Dodgshun was a young missionary full of promise, moved by love to Christ and burning zeal for the cause of missions. He went out as one of the pioneers to Central Africa, and after a weary, toilsome journey, full of incidents and perils, he reached Lake Tanganyika, which is upward of six hundred English miles to the west of Zanzibar on the West Coast of Africa, only to lie down and die. He yielded up his strength and his life for the Master's cause.

After his death, among the relics which were sent home there was a locket he had worn constantly, in which he had written the motto by which he meant to shape his course of devotion to Christ. In legible though small letters were found the words,

"GOD HELPING ME, I WILL."

Then in his diary, as if to make it all plain, he wrote the following lines, showing exactly what he meant by the motto; and happy will it be for us all if we can make the motto our own in the spirit in which this sainted man adopted it:

"GOD HELPING ME, I WILL.

"SINCE first I made this motto mine,
    How many years have come and gone!
    And still, as other years roll on,
I long to bend my will to thine.

"I felt my weakness—feel it still;
    I knew mere human strength must fail,
    But since thy power must aye prevail,
I wrote, 'God Helping me, I Will.'

"How often have my sins concealed
    The shining of thy face from me,
    Until thy grace has made me see
The light of life in Christ revealed!

"How often has my willful heart
    Repressed the right, and let me stray
    Far from the strait and narrow way
Which leads to heaven, where thou art!

"And life has had its storms and calms—
By hopes upheld, by sins opprest—
But still thou callest me to rest
Within the everlasting arms—

"To rest, but not to leave the strife;
To rest, by making efforts new
To conquer evil—to be true
To Him who lived no sluggard's life.

"Lord, shouldst thou see me standing still
While precious sheaves ungathered lie,
Say, 'Son, go labor,' and I'll cry,
'I will, God helping me—I will.'"

7 Sing, "Work, for the night is coming."
8. Prayer.
9. Some one read the following:

PART OF THE CONCERN.

A CLERGYMAN on his way to a missionary meeting overtook a boy, and asked him about the road and where he was going.

"Oh," he said, "I'm going to the meeting to hear about the missionaries."

"Missionaries!" said the minister. "What do you know about missionaries?"

"Why," said the boy, "I'm part of the concern. I've got a missionary-box, and I always go to the missionary meeting. *I belong.*"

Every child should feel that he is "part of the concern," and that his work is just as important as that of any one else. Linch-pins are little things, but if they drop out, the wagon is very likely to come to a standstill. Every pin and screw should be in working order, and every child should be able to say, "I always go to missionary meeting. Why, I'm part of the concern."

10. Another read:

LOVE MAKES THE DIFFERENCE.

James Wilson was a boy who had lately joined the Church. One day an old friend and former teacher, who had often spoken to him about becoming a Christian, met him.

"Well, James," said he, "how are you getting on?"

"Very well, sir. Why, it's just as different as can be."

"What is different?"

"Being a Christian—everything is so different from what I expected."

"Well, what did you expect?"

"Why, you see, when you used to talk to me about being a Christian I would say to myself, 'No, I can't now, for I shall have to do so many hard things that I am afraid to try it.'"

"What hard things?"

"Oh, I used to think, 'If I become a Christian I shall have to go to church and to meeting—shall have to pray and to read the Bible, and be so careful about everything.' But I find it so different to what I thought."

"Why, James, what do you mean?" asked his friend. "You *do* go to church and to meeting, and you read your Bible, and pray, and try to do what you know is right in everything, don't you?"

"Of course I do," said James, looking up to his friend with a sweet smile; "but then, you see, I *love* to do it now, and this makes all the difference. The fact is, that I love Jesus. And instead of being a burden to do anything for him, it is just the greatest pleasure I have, to do what I know he wants me to do."

Nothing in the world is so pleasant as what we do for those we really love.

11. Some one recite:

"GOD WANTS US ALL.

" God wants the boys, the merry, merry boys,
    The noisy boys, the funny boys,
      The thoughtless boys;
God wants the boys with all their joys,
    That he as gold may make them pure,
    And teach them trials to endure.
      His heroes brave
        He'll have them be,
      Fighting for truth
        And purity.
      GOD WANTS THE BOYS.

" God wants the happy-hearted girls,
    The loving girls, the best of girls,
      The worst of girls;
God wants to make the girls his pearls,
    And so reflect his holy face,
    And bring to mind his wondrous grace,
      That beautiful
        The world may be,
      And filled with love
        And purity.
      GOD WANTS THE GIRLS."

12. Sing, "More love to thee, O Christ."
13. Short address, five or ten minutes.
14. Lord's Prayer in concert.
15. *Mizpah*—" The Lord watch between me and thee when we are absent one from another."

MISSIONARY CATECHISM.

What is the great Bible command for Missions?

    Go ye into all the world and preach,
    The gospel to every creature teach!

Does this mean that all should go?

    To some it means that they should go—
    That others should their means bestow:
    To all who now enjoy the light
    The message comes, Dispel the night.

Can the children obey this command?

    Though we are young, still we can give
    A helping hand that they may live;
    Our mites we earn, and these we save
    To send the bread across the wave.

Why should you feel that these mites are acceptable to the Lord?

    Our Saviour said while here on earth,
    " A cup of water hath its worth."
    The widow's mite, when it was given,
    Rose as sweet incense unto heaven.

What is the final object for which you are working?

    That for the kingdoms of his Son
    May this world's kingdoms all be won—
    That all shall own his sovereign sway,
    And nations be born in a day.

What authority have you for believing that the whole world will be finally brought to Christ?

    The Bible tells us this is true;
    The words are sent to us and you,
    That to him every knee shall bend,
    All tongues confess him Saviour, Friend.

Should you feel grateful that you are surrounded by gospel privileges?

Yes, we should daily bless the hand
That placed us in a Christian land,
And all our grateful praises bring
To " Christ our Prophet, Priest and King."

Will you be held responsible for these blessings and for all your gifts?

Our Lord requires that these shall be
As talents returned with usury.
We all should then each gift improve,
Since he has shown such wondrous love.

THE BETHLEHEM STAR.

" Now when Jesus was born in Bethlehem of Judæa in the days of Herod the king, behold there came wise men from the east to Jerusalem, saying, Where is he that is born King of the Jews? for we have seen his star in the east, and are come to worship him."

A beautiful star of purest light
On Bethlehem rose divinely bright,
And over the infant Saviour smiled,
While angels blessed the holy child.

Chorus: Shining still, shining still,
Beautiful Bethlehem morning star.

"Lo, the star which they saw in the east went before them, till it came and stood over where the young child was."

That wonderful star, whose beams of old,
The prophets in their song foretold—
That wonderful star that came to earth,
Bright herald of the Saviour's birth.

Chorus: Shining still, etc.

"And suddenly there was with the angel a multitude of the heavenly host praising God, and saying, Glory to God in the highest, and on earth peace, good will toward men."

> O children of God, with rapture sing
> Hosanna to our Saviour King!
> Oh, joyfully sing the song again
> Of glory, peace, good-will to men!

Chorus: Shining still, etc.

(Tune in *Songs of Salvation.*)

INFANT-CLASS MISSIONARY EXERCISE.
PART I.

Congregation rise and sing—

"From Greenland's icy mountains"

(one stanza, while class take their places).

Class in Concert.—"For God so loved the world that he gave his only-begotten Son, that whosoever believeth in him should not perish, but have everlasting life."

Recitation.—"Have you heard of Jesus?" Designed to be recited by five little girls, standing in a row, each turning to the child at her left as she repeats the last two lines of her verse:

> "Little child, so bright and fair,
> Have *you* heard of Jesus?"

First little Girl.—

> "Little child, so bright and fair,
> By my pathway straying—
> Eyes of blue, and golden hair,

Pleasant face beyond compare—
Have you heard of Jesus?
Little child, so bright and fair,
Have you heard of Jesus?"

Second little Girl.—
"Yes. He was born in Bethlehem,
Cradled in a manger;
King, without a diadem;
Wise men brought him spice and gem,
Brought the little stranger.
Little child, so bright and fair,
Have *you* heard of Jesus?"

Third little Girl.—
"Yes. Little children, in his arms
He was wont to take them;
There they rested from alarms,
There they felt his tender charms;
He would ne'er forsake them.
Little child, so bright and fair,
Have *you* heard of Jesus?"

Fourth little Girl.—
"Yes. But there is a stranger tale,
Which to learn I'd have you:
How this Jesus stooped and died,
How with spear they pierced his side,
From your sins to save you.
Little child, so bright and fair,
Have *you* heard of Jesus?"

Fifth little Girl.—
"Yes. Little children, bright and fair,
He would have you love him;
From his throne he watches there;
Cast yourself upon his care;
There's no friend above him.
I'm glad these children, bright and fair

(looking down the line of children),
    Have heard so *much* of Jesus."

Chanting (tune in "Prize").—
    "Jesus, only Jesus,
      He is all we need,
    He who doth for ever
      For us intercede.

    "Jesus, gracious Jesus,
      He for us has died.
    What a gracious Saviour
      Is the Crucified!

    "Jesus, faithful Jesus,
      Ne'er will he forsake:
    From his daily presence
      May we courage take."

Chorus:
    "Jesus, blessed Jesus,
      At thy feet we fall:
    Precious Saviour, Jesus,
      Thou art all in all."

PART II.

Girl.—
    "But are there not some little ones,
      Away in their heathen homes,
    Who've never been told how Jesus
      Once said, 'Let the little children come'?

    "I'm told they have no *Bible,*
      No *holy Sabbath day,*
    No *teacher, friend, disciple,*
      To *teach them how to pray.*"

Singing, solo.—
    "Shall we whose souls are lighted," etc.

Class sing as chorus.—
    "Salvation, oh, salvation."

Part III.

Girl.—Who are the heathen?

Class in Concert.—Those who worship idols and have no knowledge of the true God.

Girl.—And do they know nothing of Jesus Christ, who came into the world to save sinners? Have they never heard that the Bible says, "*Whosoever* shall call upon the name of the Lord shall be saved"?

Class in Concert.—"How then *shall* they call on Him in whom they have not believed, and how shall they believe in Him of whom they have not heard, and how shall they *hear* without a preacher, and how shall they *preach* except they be *sent?* as it is written"—

Girl.—"How beautiful are the feet of them that preach the gospel of peace, and bring glad tidings of good things!"

Boy.—Is there not something the *children* can do to send the Bible and a preacher to those little ones over the seas?

Ans. by singing (solo and chorus, No. 27 *Primary Songs*).—

"There is something on earth for the children to do."

Girl.—What are those people called who go to teach the heathen?

Boy.—Missionaries. We have examples of them in the Bible.

Girl.—*Isaiah* heard the voice of the Lord, saying, Whom shall I send? He answered, Here am I, send me.

Boy.—The word of the Lord came unto Jonah, saying, Arise, go unto Nineveh, and preach unto it the preaching that I bid thee.

Girl.—*Christ* also sent out missionaries. "He appointed other seventy also, and sent them two and two, before his face, into every city and place whither he himself would come."

Boy.—Paul was sent to the Gentiles to open their eyes, and to turn them from darkness to light, and from the power of Satan unto God.

Girl.—Christ *himself* was a missionary. "The Son of man came not to be ministered *unto*, but to *minister*, and to give his life a ransom for many."

Boy.—*We* mean to follow Christ's example, and be missionary workers, trying to do with our might what our hands find to do.

Singing (solo and chorus, No. 24 *Primary Songs*, changing the word "pilgrim" to *worker*, thus):

"I'm a little worker."

Part IV.

Girl.—How does Christ regard what we do for him?

Class in Concert.—"Inasmuch as ye have done it unto one of the least of these my brethren, ye have done it unto me."

Boy.—We cannot *all* go to the heathen: what *can* we do?

Class in Concert.—We can "*pray* the Lord of the harvest that he would send forth laborers into the harvest."

Girl.—Is *prayer all* that is necessary?

Class in Concert.—It is *not*. We must *give*. Faith without *works* is *dead*. "Remember the words of the Lord Jesus, how he said, It is more blessed to give than to receive."

Boy.—*How* should we give?

Class.—God loveth a *cheerful* giver.

Recitation by Girl, followed by a missionary hymn.

Girl.—What petition in the Lord's Prayer refers to the heathen?

Boy.—Thy kingdom come, thy will be done in earth, as it is in heaven.

Girl.—What, then, is the duty of all, both old and young?

Class in Concert.—To *work*, *pray*, *give*, and so obey the Saviour's command, which says, "Go ye into all the world, and preach the gospel to every creature."

Congregation join children in singing,

"Waft, waft, ye winds, his story," etc.

—The Heart and Hand.

FOR A MISSION CIRCLE OF CHILDREN.

Arrangements to be Made in Advance.

CUT out from stiff card-board twelve pieces of any shape you please—a shield or a crescent, for example. They should be about eight inches in length. Cut from some bright-colored paper the twelve letters which form the word MISSIONARIES. Paste each one of these successively on the twelve bits of card-board, and attach to the corners of each a bit of bright ribbon by which to hang one letter around the neck of each of the twelve children who are to take their share in the exercises. The letters should be large, say six inches, so as to be seen distinctly at a distance. The little girls should be nearly as possible of the same height, so that when each letter hangs upon the breast they shall be in a line. Have a broad platform prepared for the children to stand on, so that they are not crowded. Finally, drill the children well in learning and reciting their verses correctly.

On the evening of the meeting have the twelve children about whose necks the twelve cards are suspended (the letters being reversed, out of sight) stand in a line in the middle of the platform. On each side stand four other children facing each other. If there are not enough in the Mission Circle for this, then let there be one child each side, instead of four, who repeats what otherwise the eight children would repeat in succession, thus:

1st Child.—
"We are taught to serve the Lord,
His precepts to obey,
To read and love his holy word,
And serve him every day."

2d, opposite Child.—
"But there are those in heathen lands,
Young children, such as we,
Who to dumb idols raise their hands,
To idols bow the knee."

No. 3, who stands next to No. 1.—
"We are taught our friends to love,
Our parents to obey—
Our enemies, if such we have,
To help in every way."

No. 4, who stands next to No. 2.—
"In heathen lands they are not taught
Gentle and kind to be,
To love each other as they ought,
Both friend and enemy."

No. 5, who stands next to No. 3.—
"We are taught to keep God's day,
The sacred day of rest;
We learn about the heavenly way
In which we may be blest."

No. 6, who stands next to No. 4.—
"The heathen child to deeds of sin,
To cruel, selfish ways,

Is left in childhood to begin,
And practice all his days."

No. 7, who stands next to No. 5.—
"Our teachers point to Jesus' life,
And teach us he must be
Our pattern in this world of strife,
Our great example he."

No. 8, who stands next to No. 6.—
"Oh, might Christ's great example be
To all the children given,
So that they all should plainly see
The road that leads to heaven!"

All of these Eight Children now repeat together.—
"What can we do to send God's word
To those who've not the message heard?
Oh, who to them will give that light
To save them from sin's cruel blight?"

The Twelve Children who have the Twelve Cards reply in Concert.—
"See! we can tell you how to give
The means to teach them how to live.
These messengers that you can send
May teach of Christ, the sinner's Friend.

Now each of these twelve children reverses in turn the card which is hung about her neck, displaying in succession the letters which form the word MISSIONARIES.

In doing this each repeats the line appropriate while turning the letter in sight, as follows (care should be taken that the children speak promptly, without undue pauses to break the sense, while turning the letter in sight):

"*M* is the letter I first turn in sight."
"*I* is the next one; I place it aright."

"*S*, though so crooked, is useful, you see;"
"And another *S* comes its companion to be."
"*I* now is repeated; before you it stands;"
"And *O* is the one that meets our demands.'
"*N* is the next letter to stand in the row;"
"And *A* is quite ready in its order to go."
"*R* will *not* be behindhand: it stands in its place;"
"And *I* comes again; I show you its face."
"*E* near the end should most properly be;"
"And *S* ends the word, which before us you see."

Now each in turn names her letter, thus spelling the word, and in concert they pronounce it—*Missionaries.*

While the children stand thus before the audience with the letters in sight a hymn on the subject of missions can be sung by all present. After this let every child upon the platform successively or in concert repeat a verse from the Scripture appropriate to the subject; the selections should be made both from the Old and New Testaments, and should be carefully *committed to memory*, so that the impression upon the child's mind may be permanent.

If among the older scholars there are any who can be nicely trained to recite a piece in reference to the wants of the heathen or our duty in respect to them, this could be appropriately done now, while as a background the children still stand with the letters which form the subject of the recitation.

We furnish the following, taken from a missionary magazine:

"THE BEST USE OF A PENNY.

"Should you wish to be told the best use of a penny,
I'll tell you a way that is better than any:
Not on apples, or cakes, or playthings to spend it,
But over the seas to the heathen to send it.

Come listen to me, and I'll tell, if you please,
Of some poor little children far over the seas.

"Their color is dark, for our God made them thus;
But he made them with bodies and feelings like us:
A soul, too, that never will die, has been given,
And there's room for these children with Jesus in heaven.
But who will now tell of such good things as these
To the poor little heathen far over the seas?

"Little boys in this land are well off indeed;
They have schools every day, where they sing, write and read;
To church they may go, and have pastors to teach
How the true way to heaven through Jesus to reach.
Yet, sad to remember, there are so few of these
For the poor little heathen far over the seas.

"Oh think, then, of this when a penny is given:
'I can help a poor child on his way home to heaven.'
Then give it to Jesus, and he will approve,
Nor scorn e'en the mite if 'tis offered in love;
And oh, when in prayer you to him bend your knees,
Remember the children far over the seas."

—*The Mission Monthly.*

OUR LITTLE SISTERS.

For Four Little Ones.

First Voice.—

"Away in the tropical meadows
 Where the wonderful Ganges swells,
'Neath the palm trees' beautiful shadows,
 My dear little sister dwells.
I have never stooped down and kissed her,
 Our arms we may never entwine,
But I know she is surely my sister,
 Since God is her Father and mine.

"But oh, ere a year is ended
  She may sink in a terrible grave,
And her last little cry may be blended
  With the rush of the Ganges' wave;
For they tell me the heathen mother
  Her babe to the river-god throws;
O'er many a sister and brother
  The terrible Ganges flows."

Second Voice.—

"Where the billowy waves are swelling,
  Oh, thousands of leagues from here,
In an isle of the ocean dwelling,
  I too have a sister dear.
I never have stooped down and kissed her,
  Our arms may never entwine;
But I know she is surely my sister,
  Since God is her Father and mine.

"No one in the isle is fairer
  Than she, nor so happy and gay;
But oh, I'm afraid they will bear her
  To the terrible shrine away;
And my sister may now be seeing
  The last of her days so fair,
For many a human being
  Is offered to idols there."

Third Voice.—

"I too have a sister; I love her,
  Though God in his wisdom has made
The hue her young face and form over
  Of Africa's tawniest shade.
I never have stooped down and kissed her
  Our arms we may never entwine;
But I know she is surely my sister,
  Since God is her Father and mine.

"There is sorrow in every feature,
  And pain in my sister's soul;

She is bowing before a creature
    All loathsome and grim and foul;
For Africa lies in darkness
    So thick that it seems to me
My poor little African sister
    The morning will never see."

Fourth Voice.—
"Oh, hear us, our fathers and mothers!
    Our sorrowing spirits cry,
And help to our sisters and brothers
    Send quickly before they die—
Send and tell them the good Shepherd leads us
    To God, the kind Father above,
And how from the heavens he heeds us,
    And looks down upon us with love."

All.—
"For our spirits all stoop down and kiss them,
    We entwine them with love and with prayers!
In heaven we must meet and not miss them,
    Since God is our Father and theirs."—*Selected.*

NOTHING TO DO.

First Scholar.—
"Nothing to do in this world of ours,
    Where the weeds spring up 'mid the fairest flowers,
    Where smiles have only a fitful play,
    Where hearts are breaking every day?"

Second Scholar.—
"'Nothing to do'? Thou Christian soul,
    Wrapping thee round in thy selfish stole,
    If with the garments of sloth and sin,
    Christ, thy Lord, hath a kingdom to win."

Third Scholar.—
"'Nothing to do'? There are prayers to lay
On the altar of incense day by day;
There are foes to meet within and without,
There is error to conquer, strong and stout."

Fourth Scholar.—
"'Nothing to do'? There are minds to teach
The simplest forms of Christian speech;
There are hearts to lure with loving wile
From the grimmest haunts of sin's defile."

Fifth Scholar.—
"'Nothing to do'? There are lambs to feed,
The precious hope of the Church's need,
Strength to be borne to the weak and faint,
Vigils to keep with the doubting saint."

Sixth Scholar.—
"'Nothing to do'? There are heights to attain,
Where Christ is transfigured yet again,
Where earth will fade in the vision sweet,
And the soul pass on with wingèd feet."

Whole Class, in Concert.—
"'Nothing to do'? and thy Saviour said,
'Follow thou me in the path I tread.'
Lord, lend thy help the journey through,
Lest, faint, we cry, 'So much to do!'"—*Selected*

OUR BEST FOR THE MASTER.

By Mrs. S. C. Jayne.

Long the heathen mother lingered
Near the couch where quiet lay
Her twin babes, in gentle slumber
Sleeping peaceful hours away—

One a boy of beauteous features,
  Perfect form and budding mind,
But the other all disfigured,
  Almost idiot and blind.

Sad the mother's heart with weeping,
  For her idol god demands
One of these dear babes, a victim
  Sacrificed by her own hands.
Well she knows that naught unsightly
  Will the cruel Gunga please,
That her brightest, fairest treasure
  Only will her wrath appease;
Trembling, faltering, then she seizes
  Him, the dimpled, laughing-eyed,
Hastens where the Ganges floweth,
  Bravely throws him in the tide.

O poor stricken, heathen mother!
  If the Christian's faith were given,
You would see the dear, good Jesus
  Reaching down to earth from heaven—
With his arms of love and pity
  Folded round your darling, rise,
Bearing safe his little spirit
  To the nursery of the skies.

Sisters, can you hope to fathom
  Half that mother's wondering joy
When she fully comprehendeth
  She again will see her boy?
Send this knowledge to her quickly,
  Heal her bleeding, broken heart,
Tell her in the home of heaven
  Loved ones meet no more to part.

Did you list the earnest pleading
  As it came direct to you,
"Give, oh give, this gospel to us!
  We would learn of Jesus too;

If we may not worship with you,
If too vile and poor we are,
Oh, kind lady, when you enter,
Will you leave the door ajar?"

Send this knowledge to them quick'y,
Neither gold nor silver spare,
But let every dollar of it be
Well wrapped up in faith and prayer.

RECITATION.

[THE following may be made very effective by having the verses of the "Missionary Hymn" sung, the other stanzas being *recited:*]

THE MISSIONARY HYMN.

I.

"Now let us sing," the preacher said;
And as the book he lifted;
Across his patient, careworn face
A bright expression drifted.
Stood listening the forest trees
Around that cabin lowly;
Halted the wolf and snuffed the breeze,
On which came faintly, slowly,

" From Greenland's icy mountains,
From India's coral strand,
Where Afric's sunny fountains
Roll down their golden sand;
From many an ancient river,
From many a palmy plain,
They call us to deliver
Their land from error's chain."

II.

" Now let us sing;" and at the word,
From prairie-pulpit uttered,

Like rustling leaves before a shower
  The white-winged pages fluttered;
Then burst the hymn; the long grass waved
  The grouse stirred in its cover,
Still stood the deer with head erect,
  Up sprang the startled plover:

"What though the spicy breezes
  Blow soft o'er Ceylon's isle;
Though every prospect pleases,
  And only man is vile;
In vain with lavish kindness
  The gifts of God are strown:
The heathen in his blindness
  Bows down to wood and stone."

III.

"Now let us sing:" the city throng,
  Crowding around the preacher,
The tale of heathen weal and woe
  Had heard from earnest teacher.
The breath of organ, chant of choir,
  In grand reverberation,
Shook transept, nave and vaulted roof,
  With fervent deprecation:

"Shall we, whose souls are lighted
  By wisdom from on high,
Shall we to men benighted,
  The lamp of life deny?
Salvation! oh, salvation!
  The joyful sound proclaim,
Till earth's remotest nation
  Has learned Messiah's name."

IV.

Where'er is heard our English tongue,
  From continent to ocean,
The wondrous hymn, those burning lines,
  Are sung with deep emotion;

From distant isles, from China seas,
  Resolve and courage bringing;
From Saxon, Indian, African,
  To-day the words are ringing:

' Waft, waft, ye winds, his story,
  And you, ye waters, roll,
Till, like a sea of glory,
  It spreads from pole to pole—
Till o'er our ransomed nature
  The Lamb for sinners slain,
Redeemer, King, Creator,
  In bliss returns to reign."

V.

O lyric grand! thy noble words,
  All noble deeds suggesting,
Have ever stirred the Christian heart
  To work and toil unresting;
And till the Church's fight is fought
  Thine utterances glorious,
A battle-cry, a trumpet-call,
  Shall lead the host victorious.—*Selected.*

(*By special permission.*)

THE MISSIONARY CLOCK.

By Mrs. Louise Kinney.

[THERE should be a large clock-face constructed of pasteboard, large enough to be seen distinctly from any part of the room in which the performance takes place. The numbers on the face of the clock are represented by the texts of Scripture on which the verses are based—1 being a text of one word; 2, a text of two words, and so on up to 12. Arrange the texts upon the face of the clock in such a manner as to form convergent lines toward the centre. The hands must be made to move easily, both pointing to 12 at the beginning of the exercise. The introductory verse is first recited, without changing the hands. The hour "one" is then struck, with a small bell, by some one in the rear. As the hour strikes let one of the children advance to the clock *from the right*, move the hour-hand forward to "one," recite the text and the corresponding verse, and then remain standing at the right of the clock. "Two" is then struck with the bell. Let the next one advance from the *left*, move the hand forward to number "two" upon the clock, repeat her text and verse, and remain standing upon the left of the clock. Let the next approach from the right again, the one following from the left, and so on, until at the end the Band forms a semicircle facing the audience. The texts and verses may be recited by different ones if the Band is large and it is desired to have many take part in the exercise. The prayer at the close is to be repeated in concert by the Band, either kneeling or standing with bowed heads and folded hands. After the prayer, the hymn "Whiter than the Snow" (Palmer's *Songs of Love*), sung by the Band, makes a beautiful and effective ending.]

"Tick-tock, tick-tock!"
Hear the Missionary Clock.
It hath a voice for every hour,
Words of soft, persuasive power.
Would you know what it is saying
In its ceaseless, solemn swaying?—
"Go ye into all the earth!
Preach the gospel's priceless worth
Unto every longing soul,
Till from pole to farthest pole
Every creature knows the story,
Bows before the Lord of Glory."

1.   ["Come." Rev. 22 : 17.]
"Tick-tock, tick-tock!"
Hear the Missionary Clock.
"One" it striketh; sweet and clear
Falls its summons on mine ear:
"Come! thy Father calleth for thee;
Come! thy Saviour yearneth for thee;
Come! oh, give me now thy heart
While in life's fair morn thou art!
Come!" it calls with silvery chime;
"Now is the accepted time."

2. ["Follow me." Luke 9 : 59.]

"Tick-tock, tick-tock!"
Hear the Missionary Clock.
"Two" it striketh: "Follow me!
I, the Lord, am leading thee.
Though the way seem dark and dreary,
Though thy feet be often weary,
Though I lead through desert sands
Or the gloom of heathen lands;
Though the end thou canst not see,
Take thy cross and follow me."

3. ["Pray without ceasing." 1 Thess. 5 : 17.]

"Tick-tock, tick-tock!"
Hear the Missionary Clock.
"Three" it striketh, true and strong;
Prayer the burden of its song:
"Pray, oh, pray!" 'tis ever saying;
"Pray, oh, pray, nor cease thy praying:
Pray at morn, at noon, at night;
Pray to know and to do the right;
Pray for guidance, strength and peace;
Pray, nor e'er thy praying cease!"

4. ["Keep yourselves from idols." 1 John 5 : 21.]

"Tick-tock, tick-tock!"
Hear the Missionary Clock.
"Four" it striketh: "Let there be
In thy heart no gods but me.
Keep yourselves from idols, tearing
From my throne all loves, nor sparing
E'en the dearest, if it be
Growing 'twixt thy love and me;
For a jealous God am I,
Yearning o'er you lest ye die."

5. ["The field is the world." Matt. 13 : 38.]

"Tick-tock, tick-tock!"
Hear the Missionary Clock.

"Five" it striketh: "Lift thine eyes,
 Lo, the field before thee lies!
  Go thou forth with seed for sowing;
  Where the Eastern skies are glowing,
  Where the Western rivers flow:
  O'er the broad earth shalt thou go.
 Haste the Master's work to do;
 The field is broad, the laborers few."

6. ["Thrust in thy sickle and reap." Rev. 14 : 16.]
  "Tick-tock, tick-tock!"
   Hear the Missionary Clock.
"Six" it striketh, full and deep:
"Thrust thy sickle in and reap.
   Lo! afar the fields are gleaming
   White unto the harvest, seeming
   Ready for the reapers; why
   Stand you thus so idly by?
 Rouse ye, dreamers, from your sleep;
 Thrust your sickles in and reap!"

7. ["Come over into Macedonia and help us." Acts 16 : 9.]
  "Tick-tock, tick-tock!"
   Hear the Missionary Clock.
"Seven" it striketh; and its call,
 Piercing, urgent, comes to all:
   "Come and help us!" they are crying,
   "Come and help, for we are dying;
    Give your prayers or give your gold,
    Labor, time nor strength withhold;
 Help us howsoe'er you may;
 Only come and help, we pray!"

8. ["I will require my flock at their hand." Ezek. 34 : 10.]
  "Tick-tock, tick-tock!"
   Hear the Missionary Clock.
"Eight" it striketh: words of fire:
"At thy hand I will require

All my flock! Oh, heed the warning!
Turn not hence with idle scorning;
Unto you the trust is given;
Ye must point the way to heaven.
Go, and seek, and find, and keep;
Ye are shepherds of my sheep."

9. ["I shall give thee the heathen for thine inheritance." Ps. 2 : 8.]

"Tick-tock, tick-tock!"
Hear the Missionary Clock.
"Nine" it striketh; ere 'tis done
Hear the promise to the Son :
"I will ne'er forsake nor leave thee;
Ask of me and I will give thee
All the heathen for thine own;
They shall bow before my throne;
All the earth, from sea to sea,
Thine inheritance shall be."

10. ["In due season we shall reap if we faint not." Gal. 6 : 9.]

"Tick-tock, tick-tock!"
Hear the Missionary Clock.
"Ten" it striketh; comfort sweet,
Grace and strength to faltering feet :
"Weary not in thy well-doing,
Day by day thy strength renewing;
In due season ye shall reap
If ye faint not; therefore keep
Bravely on, with steadfast heart;
Trust in God, and do thy part."

11. ["Believe on the Lord Jesus Christ, and thou shalt be saved." Acts 16 : 31.]

"Tick-tock, tick-tock!"
Hear the Missionary Clock.
"Eleven" it striketh; solemnly
Comes its charge to you and me:
"But one name on earth is given;
But one way that leads to heaven:

Jesus Christ, the Father's Son—
    He will save, and he alone;
By the blood which he hath shed
Ye are ransomed from the dead."

12. ["I am with you alway, even unto the end of the world." Matt 28:20.]

      "Tick-tock, tick-tock!"
      Hear the Missionary Clock.
  "Twelve" it striketh; and its beat
  Makes the mystic round complete:
      "Lo! I'm with you alway, even
         To the very gates of heaven.
      I will strengthen thee and bless;
      I will comfort in distress;
  All thy way I will befriend;
  I will keep thee to the end."

    Thus the Clock with every hour
    Speaks with soft, persuasive power.
    Ever, through the silence falling,
    We may hear it, calling, calling;
    Even now it seems to say,
  "Little children, let us pray."

      Heavenly Father, hear us now,
        As before thy throne we bow!
    May we feel thy dear hand pressing
    On each bowed young head in blessing—
    Hear thy voice, in tenderest tone,
    Calling to us, one by one!
        May we help thy name to carry,
        Each a little missionary,
        Telling of our Saviour's love,
        Pointing to the home above!
    Cleanse our hearts before we go;
    Wash us whiter than the snow;
    Bless us all, we pray again,
      For dear Jesus's sake. AMEN.

(*By special permission.*)
SONG OF THE "WILLING WORKERS."
By Mrs. Louise Kinney.

[The first six verses should be recited by different members of the Band. The remaining four are to be sung, either by the Band in concert or by individual members, the Band joining in tne chorus at the close of each verse. Sing to tune "Only a little Sparrow," in *Sunshine*, by Mr. P. P. Bliss.]

1. Only a little penny!
   Yet with assurance sweet,
  Fearing no scorn, we lay it
   Down at dear Jesus' feet,
  Saving for him a portion
   Out of our slender store;
  Joyfully giving our pennies,
   If we can do no more.

2. Only a little penny!
   Poor in itself we know;
  Yet, if we patiently gather,
   Pennies to pounds may grow;
  Little by little increasing
   Unto a goodly sum,
  Just as the tiny streamlets
   Rivers and lakes become.

3. Only a little minute!
   Gone like some swift-winged bird,
  The sweep of whose airy pinions
   The silence scarce has stirred.
  Only a little minute!
   Yet 'tis a precious gem
  Which the dear Lord hath lent us,
   That we may use for him.

4. Only a little minute!
   Yet there is time to lift
  A whispered prayer to Jesus,
   Winning the Spirit's gift—

Time for a word of comfort,
  Time for a kindly deed,
Time by the way to scatter
  Many a precious seed.

5. Only ten little fingers!
    Not very strong, 'tis true;
  Yet there is work for Jesus
    Such little hands may do.
  What though it be but humble,
    Winning no word of praise,
  We are but little children,
    Working in little ways.

6. Only ten little fingers!
    But little things may grow,
  And little hands, now helpless,
    Will not be always so;
  And, if we train them early
    Unto his work alone,
  They will do greater service
    When they are stronger grown.

7. Only a band of children!
    Sitting at Jesus' feet,
  Fitting ourselves to enter
    Into his service sweet.
  Softly his voice is calling:
    "Little one, come unto me!
  Stay not, though weak and helpless;
    Child, I have need of *thee!*"

  Chorus: Only a band of children!
        Sitting at Jesus' feet,
      Fitting ourselves to enter
        Into his service sweet.

8. Take us, dear Saviour, take us
    Into thy heavenly fold!
  Keep our young feet from straying
    Out in the dark and cold;

Call us thy "Little Helpers,"
  Glad in thy work to share;
Make us thine own dear children,
  Worthy thy Name to bear.

9. Only a band of children!
  Sitting at Jesus' feet,
Fitting ourselves to enter
  Into his service sweet;
Seeking his light to guide us
  Wherever the way is dim,
Learning his beautiful lessons,
  Longing to be like him.

10. Oh, with pure hearts and lowly
  Help us, dear Lord, to go;
Bearing the glad, sweet story
  Unto sad hearts below;
And reaching the pearly portals,
  May the welcome sweet be given:
"Pass through the gates, my children;
  Of such is the kingdom of heaven."

(*By special permission.*)

THE PLEA OF THE NATIONS.

By Mrs. Louise Kinney.

[THE heathen nations are personated by young ladies or children. Each advances to the front in turn and presents her plea. If desired, upon retiring the hymn "Behold the Nations Kneeling" may be sung.]

Japan.—
"Across the sea, full many a mile,
From far Japan's sea-girded isle,
I come, O Christian friends! to plead
My country's dire and urgent need:
Teach us to tear our idols down,
And give unto *your* God the crown."

China.—

> "*I* come from China. Dark and deep
> Pacific's rolling billows sweep
> 'Twixt your fair land and mine, where now
> Unnumbered millions blindly bow,
> And prayers are poured and vows are paid
> To gods which their own hands have made."

Siam.—

> "*I* come from shores of far Siam.
> Our land is fair with fig and palm;
> But darkness deeper than the night
> Enshrouds her hills and valleys bright.
> Oh, for the Christian's light to shine
> Upon this poor loved land of mine!"

India.—

> "*I* come from India's ancient land.
> Her forests, vales and mountains grand
> With idol temples are defiled;
> The air is rent with mournings wild;
> And suffering women live and die
> In hopeless, hapless misery."

Persia.—

> "From Persia's sunny vales *I* come.
> No longer may our lips be dumb!
> The days and years are fleeting by,
> And we in heathen darkness die.
> Oh, haste the Bread of Life to give,
> That Persia too may eat and live!"

Syria.—

> "From Syria's sacred shores *I* come—
> The land *your* Saviour called his own,
> Yet where his holy feet once trod
> They know not of the living God!
> O Christian people! heed our call;
> Teach us of Him who died for all."

Africa.—

"From Afric's darkened shores am *I:*
Hark! hear ye not that mournful cry?
There human blood is daily shed,
And living souls are as the dead.
Oh, haste and help to free our land
From Error's dread, despotic hand."

South America.—

"Not from the distant Orient *I:*
Our land lies 'neath your own fair sky.
Yet South America has needs,
And earnestly, O Christians! pleads
For help to break the chains that bind,
And life's immortal way to find."

North American Indian.—

"*This* noble land *I* call my home,
And free its hills and forests roam.
But I have heard the white man pray
And seek to know the living way.
Oh, come and teach the Indian brave
How your Great Spirit waits to save.'

Mexico.—

"From Mexico's hill-girded shores
I come, a suppliant at your doors.
Haste, with the Spirit's flaming sword;
Haste, in the name of Christ the Lord;
And help our fettered land to free
From Rome's dark craft and tyranny."

(*By special permission.*)

A MISSIONARY HYMN.

By Mrs. Louise Kinney.

1. Behold the nations kneeling
    'Neath far-off Eastern skies!

They call to us appealing:
  Oh hear their mournful cries.
"Our land," they say, "is shrouded
  In darkness and in gloom;
Our eyes, with tears beclouded,
  Look forth to hopeless doom."

2. Hark! hark! what strains of anguish
    Seem mingling with that cry!—
"Must we, unaided, languish?
    All unforgiven die?
  Our gods, they do not answer;
    In vain for help we sue;
  Oh tell us of *your* Saviour!
    Will he not save *us* too?"

3 O Christians! do ye hear it,
    That cry from o'er the sea?
  The swift winds haste to bear it,
    Yet slow to help are ye.
  Arouse ye from your slumbers;
    The time wears fast away,
  And souls in countless numbers
    Are perishing to-day.

SONG AND RECITATION.

```
┌─────────────────────────────────────┐
│                                     │
│   SHINE                             │
│   SERVE    FOR JESUS.               │
│   SPEAK                             │
│                                     │
└─────────────────────────────────────┘
```

(*To be printed on a Blackboard.*)

Recitation.— " Jesus bids us shine
  With a pure, clear light,
Like a little candle
  Burning in the night.
In a world of darkness
  So we must shine,
You in your small corner,
  And I in mine.

" Jesus bids us shine,
  First of all, for him;
Well he sees and knows it
  If our light grow dim.
He looks down from heaven
  To see us shine,
You in your small corner,
  And I in mine.

" Jesus bids us shine
  Then for all around:
Many kinds of darkness
  In the world are found—
Sin and want and sorrow;
  So we must shine,
You in your small corner,
  And I in mine."

Recite.—" Let your light so shine before men, that they may see your good works, and glorify your Father which is in heaven." Matt. 5 : 16.

Sing.— " We'll gird our loins, my brethren dear,
  Our distant home discerning;
Our absent Lord has left us word,
  Let every lamp be burning.

Chorus: " For oh, we stand on Jordan's strand;
  Our friends are passing over,
And, just before, the shining shore
  We may almost discover."

Recite.—"If any man serve me, let him follow me; and where I am, there shall also my servant be; if any man serve me, him will my Father honor." John 12 : 26.

Sing.— "Work, for the night is coming,
　　Work through the sunny noon;
　Fill brightest hours with labor;
　　Rest comes sure and soon.
　Give every flying minute
　　Something to keep in store;
　Work, for the night is coming,
　　When man works no more."

Recite.—"My mouth shall speak the praise of the Lord." Ps. 145 : 21.

Sing.—"Never be afraid to speak for Jesus;
　　Think how much a word can do;
　Never be afraid to own your Saviour,
　　He who loves and cares for you.

Chorus: "Never be afraid, never be afraid,
　　Never, never, never;
　Jesus is your loving Saviour,
　　Therefore never be afraid."

Recite in Concert.—
　"Jesus, show us how to be
　　Brightly shining lights for thee.

　"Show us how to serve thee here,
　　E'en on earth, our Saviour dear.

　"May we speak for thee each day
　　Words of kindness by the way."
　　　　—*Children's Work for Children.*

BIOGRAPHICAL EXERCISE.

[This exercise was arranged for a Band at Rock Spring, Pa., by an invalid, and may readily suggest similar ones on other topics.]

Who was Fidelia Fiske?
An American missionary to Persia.

Early home?
A one-story farm-house among the hills of Massachusetts.

Parents?
Intelligent and pious—took special pains to instruct their family in the Bible.

Religious impressions?
In early childhood religious truth impressed her; she united with the church at fifteen.

Mental qualities?
In the country schools she thoroughly mastered the branches taught—was more fond of conquering difficulties herself than of being helped over them.

Reading?
She early read all the excellent books of her father's library.

Interest in missions?
While a little girl she eagerly heard letters read from her uncle, a missionary in Palestine. She once told her mother that she had been playing missionary, and had been to Jerusalem on a wheelbarrow. She also read mission journals with great delight.

Determination to go to Persia?
Her note to Miss Lyon simply said, "If considered worthy I would like to go."

Consent of her mother?
Saturday, P. M., Miss Lyon and herself were in an open sleigh; thirty miles; upset in snow-drifts; reached Shelbourne at eleven at night. Before the next

evening her mother said to her, "Go, my child, go."

From what port did she sail?
Boston.
When?
1843.
Age?
Twenty-seven.
How long in reaching Trebizond?
Two months.
Where is Trebizond?
To what Persian city bound?
Oroomiah.
Distance from Trebizond to Oroomiah?
Eight hundred miles.
How travel?
How many missionaries?
Six, who, with those in charge of horses and baggage, made a company of twenty on horseback.
What did Miss Fiske write home?
"Being all mounted, we wished you could see us and enjoy our happiness."
What of the route?
Mountainous; Koordish robbers; no hotels or comfortable farm-houses to entertain them; they carried tents and provisions with them.
Why willing to endure such hardships?
How long in reaching Oroomiah?
One month; three from Boston.
Among what people did she labor?
Among women. Often found working in field with babe on back: evenings getting supper for husband, taking his leavings; often beaten and driven away.
Dwellings?
Single room; mud floor; opening in roof serves for

window and chimney; beds, a few quilts on floor; houses and people covered with vermin.

What did Miss Fiske establish at Oroomiah?

Were her pupils from such homes as described?

What did she say of them when first taken as boarders?

Filthy as beasts; they lie as fast as they can speak.

Why was she pleased to teach children so disagreeable?

What did she teach in her seminary?

First the Bible, two hours each day; secular branches as in our schools; housework; the boarders did their own cooking, washing, etc.

Were not her labors more arduous than with our teachers?

Why did she visit many towns?

To read the Bible and hold prayer-meetings.

Did she think a missionary lady should be a good house-keeper?

She writes: "I am as surely doing missionary work when providing good food as when holding a prayer-meeting, for a missionary's usefulness depends much on health, and health on suitable food."

Can we serve God in the kitchen as well as in the closet?

What of her vacations?

She had sometimes charge of her girls all vacation, often superintending repairs of building.

When English and Russian commissioners to the Persian court were entertained by Dr. Perkins, what impression did Miss Fiske make?

She commanded the high respect of the distinguished nobles by showing herself equal to any position in the social circle.

What does Dr. Perkins say of her?

"Our dear sister is as gifted in entertaining princes as in sitting on a mud floor teaching degraded women; with like ease she cares for her house and school and directs a dozen men repairing the building." So Fidelia Fiske was teacher and housekeeper; a mother to her pupils, providing their food and clothes; conducted religious meetings among her sex; much in the sick-room; wrote many letters to home friends; often had charge of men working on her school-building.

Why was it necessary that one delicate woman should have charge of such varied work?

"The harvest was great, but the laborers few."

Is it not still so, and to-day are not many noble missionaries overtaxed?

Was not Miss Fiske wonderfully gifted by nature and grace?

Are talent and education as necessary to a missionary as piety?

To all her labors what did Fidelia Fiske add?

Unceasing prayer with and for her pupils, and constant looking for God to fulfill his promise.

What did she write home?

"I gave up America for Christ, and to Christ I look for success."

What of her success?

Year after year God visited her school and renewed many hearts.

What was the evidence of this?

The little girls were so anxious about their souls as to be often unable to study or eat; uninvited they would come in groups of twenty to Miss Fiske to talk about Christ.

What was remarkable in the young converts?

Their prayerfulness, often having little prayer-meetings. Miss Fiske was often deeply moved by hearing their young voices in closet prayer at a late hour of the night.

Were they concerned for others?

They held prayer-meetings for the conversion of their parents.

What of a rough mountaineer who visited his daughter in the school?

The little girls formed a circle round him, and as one and another plead with God for his soul the strong man wept, and soon found Christ.

How only can you get a correct idea of Fidelia Fiske?

By reading her life, which abounds in thrilling incidents.

What of her last communion in Persia?

She sat down at the Lord's table with ninety-three Nestorian women, with all of whom but one she had at some time talked and prayed.

How many Nestorian women were Christians when she went to Persia?

Not one. We cannot all be missionaries, but if this society supports missions by money and prayer, is it not doing missionary work as truly as the laborers on the field?

How long was Fidelia Fiske in Persia?

Fifteen years.

GOING TO PERSIA.

[THE members of the Band are seated in groups, sewing, talking, etc., when two tardy ones, Kate and Annie, enter.]

Kate.—Oh, girls, we've some news for you! You remember Fanny Evart, who graduated at Vassar last year, and who has this winter been studying music and painting in New York?

Annie (interrupting).—We met her as we were coming this afternoon, and she told us she had just come home to get ready to go to Persia as a missionary. Isn't that the strangest news?

Carrie.—Nonsense, Annie! the idea of her giving up her beautiful home and leaving all her friends! I can't believe it.

Kate.—You will believe it when you see her; and when we told her our Band met this afternoon she said she would come over and tell us all about it. Ah! here she comes.

Fanny.—Has Annie told you that I am going to Persia? I think she has, for you all look astonished, I see. You never thought such a high-flyer as I, would ever do missionary work, did you?

Sarah.—Why, Fanny, I never supposed anything less than a life in Washington would satisfy your ambition.

Bertha.—Oh, girls, just fancy Fanny Evart dressed in anything but the latest style! think of her surrounded by thirty or forty uncouth little Nestorian children!—Shall you teach them painting, Fan?

Emma.—I should think there were others that could go instead of you—those that haven't any friends nor so much to give up as you.

Fanny.—Why, girls, how can you talk so? Does the Bible say, "Go, ye who are friendless and poor, ye who thereby make no sacrifices?" How many, think you, would go? I feel that it is a glorious work, and, though one of sacrifices, one of great recompense. I may be poorly fitted for the work, but I can give myself to Jesus, and be glad to do in a feeble way what otherwise might not be done at all.

Agnes.—I think Fanny is right; and, girls, this criticism of mission-power that is often made in a depreciating tone is cruelly unjust and untrue.

Minnie.—As a class, the missionaries are obliged to be, by the necessities of the case, men of training as well as heart. Let the doubtful attempt the attainment of sufficient Arabic or Indian learning to preach the gospel readily in the native dialects of Asia or Africa.

Sarah (pointing out the route on a map).—If I were going to be a missionary I wouldn't go to Persia. Do you know how long and tedious the journey is? For weeks tossed on the ocean and sea, then a journey of four weeks from Trebizond to Oroomiah upon a camel's back, over mountains, through deserts and across bridgeless rivers!

Bertha.—Persia, consequently, is so shut in that our missionaries there scarcely ever see American travelers. Now, when trips across the Continent and around the world are not uncommon, our missionaries in China and Japan may hope to have their hearts cheered occasionally by the sight of some friend.

Emma.—The people, too, are perfectly uncivilized. Why, they live in mud huts without any windows; eat with their fingers, sitting on the floor; and women are treated with no more kindness and consideration than cattle! Every form of iniquity prevails: lying is universal. The government of the country is despotic, a coarse, degraded shah ruling the people, with no desire to lift them from their wretched condition.

Fanny.—This is all true, but can nothing be done for these degraded ones? Much has already been accomplished, and a thousand-fold more may be. Do you know that it is only forty years since the American Board sent a missionary to the Nestorians? Through the efforts of missionaries the Scriptures have been translated, schools established, churches organized and a native ministry trained, by which the gospel is now preached to the people, and, as a result, thousands have been converted.

Kate.—I never was so interested in missions as now, and it seems as if there never was so much accomplished. Papa was reading only last evening the progress Japan is making. The government, which has adopted the Christian Sabbath, not only amply protects our missionaries, but is now considering the question of giving all religions full liberty of worship. The country seems ready to pass at once from the fourteenth into the nineteenth century.

Annie.—No less than forty thousand children of the Fiji Islanders are now in Sunday-school, and thousands of the people are consistent Christians, yet it is but forty years since these people were cannibals.

Julia.—In Madagascar the whole land is open to the missionaries, idolatry is overthrown and Christianity is proclaimed to be the religion of the people.

Bertha.—This missionary work always seemed to me incomprehensible. I never could get interested in the heathen—never see how anything could be accomplished, the field is so large and laborers so few. Why, if all the Christians of America would start out and try and christianize the heathen, I should feel that something could be done; but now only a few hundreds of missionaries to millions of people!

Agnes.—You remind me of the man I read of the other day who had twelve children, and wouldn't let any of them go to school till all were old enough; for then, he said, he could see that a great and rapid work was being accomplished.

Minnie.—Suppose Columbus had waited till all his countrymen were fired with his enthusiasm and were ready to go with him; when, think you, would our America have been discovered?

Fanny.—You forget that it is not intended that this work shall be done wholly and directly by missionaries sent by us. The converts made become preachers among their own people, and very faithful and efficient ones too; and so we hope at no very distant day the work will be left wholly to natives.

Kate.—Nine-tenths of the work now being done in Burmah is in the hands of native preachers.

Annie.—In a school of Massachusetts there are now numbers of young men being educated and fitted for missionaries at the expense of their own government: isn't it wonderful?

Carrie (lazily).—Well, I don't know but I am persuaded there is work to do, and somebody ought to do it; but I don't think I am quite ready to start for Persia or any other heathen land.—Are you, Mary?—There is enough to do right here at home, it seems to me.

Mary.—I think there is a great deal that we can do at home; but let us not be of the multitude who excuse themselves from helping on the work of foreign missions because there is so much wickedness in our own land. There will always be those who *might* hear the gospel, but *will not*.

Minnie.—That's right, Mary; if there are millions of people in heathen darkness who have not the gospel and know nothing of Christ and his salvation, are we not responsible if we do not go or help send substitutes to carry the glad news?

Agnes.—We must not do less, but more, each year, as new fields are being opened to us, and the cry, "Come over and help us," sounds louder and louder. Let us promise that we will the coming year do more than ever before.

Answer (from all).—We will!—*Good Times.*

What do the heathen worship?
Idols of silver and gold, the work of men's hands.

Describe them.

They have mouths, but they *speak* not; *eyes* have they, but they *see* not; they have *ears*, but they *hear* not; *noses* have they, but they *smell* not; *feet* have they, but they *walk* not.

Who are like them?

They that make them are like unto them. So is every one that trusteth in them.

POLITICAL CHANGES OF THE WORLD,

AND

THEIR EFFECT UPON MISSIONS.

Mamie.—Another new year has dawned upon us, and the old year has gone up with its record to God. Let us look back upon the great world and see what things God has been doing to advance his cause.

Mollie.—I know we have many beautiful promises, such as these: "I will give thee the heathen for thine inheritance, and the uttermost parts of the earth for thy possession;" and "The kingdoms of this world are become the kingdoms of our Lord and of his Christ;" and "His dominion shall be from sea to sea, and from the river, even to the ends of the earth."

Mamie.—The Spirit of God seems truly to be moving upon the waters, and the battles being fought are those of faiths and systems and ideas. The sleep of ages is being broken. May the Sun of Righteousness break away the mists and bring the clear light of God's truth to all nations!

Mollie.—In our own country the Indians, so long existing as a distinct nation, have adhered to the religion of their fathers to a great extent, and only through the long and faithful work of the missionary have some been brought to Christ. *This year* opens a *new* path of freedom for them. It is the policy of our government to do away with the tribal and reservation system, making every man responsible to himself and to his God, instead of to his tribe; also advancing education by furnishing schools. God seems to be sending other nations to our shores to be fed with the heavenly manna, for it is noted that thousands a day have landed here. Our outlook as a nation is peaceful, and, save in one respect, is favorable for the progress of God's kingdom.

Mamie.—What cloud do you see on the horizon?

Mollie.—The recent action of our government in respect to Chinese immigration.

Mamie.—Let us remember the promise, "The crooked shall be made straight, and the rough places plain, and the glory of the Lord shall be revealed, and all flesh shall see it together." What may be said of the lands across the sea?

Mollie.—In Japan and China "the day breaketh, the shadows are fleeing away, and the mountain-tops have caught the rays of the Sun of Righteousness."

Mamie.—India has long been the stronghold of idolatry, the testing-field of all the great religions—Buddhism, Brahminism, Mohammedanism.

Mollie.—What have they done for that country?

Mamie.—They have held the land in darkness and the women in slavery. England, through her avarice, in taking possession of the government has opened a way for the missionaries, so that to-day it is recognized that the missionary force has proved a pacificator and a conservator. One of their papers declared that this alone kept the East India Company from making shipwreck of the splendid British possessions.

Mollie.—The European missionary is daily becoming

a more important link between the government and the people. He is confided in by all people of all ranks, and is often able to do what the government with its mere professions of neutrality cannot effect. Prominent natives testify that it is the Bible that will sooner or later regenerate this land.

Mamie.—Tell of the wicked king of Burmah.

Mollie.—He was stricken with disease, and for its cure his superstitions demanded the sacrifice of human blood; so he laid upon the heathen altar one thousand human beings, including nearly all of his near relatives. To appease the wrath of his people, the English government interfered and put the king under bonds. God may use this wickedness for his own honor and glory by thus bringing this otherwise unnoticed kingdom before the world.

Mamie.—We turn from this dark picture to the bright future of Siam, where Buddhism has had more absolute sway than in any other country, and where the people have, as is spoken of in Rom. 1, "changed the glory of the incorruptible God into an image like to corruptible man, and to birds, and four-footed beasts, and creeping things"—where there has been no home, where woman has been a drudge and many of the people in slavery. To-day we can rejoice that the late king was a man of progress, and that his son, the present king, received an English education.

Mollie.—He is, I believe, next to the mikado of Japan in his earnestness for the civilization of his people, and adopts the European dress. He has given one thousand dollars, and his nobles twelve hundred, toward a new school-building for our mission, proclaimed religious liberty to the Laos, secured the observance of the Sabbath, and made one of the missionaries superintendent of public instruction, with a salary of five thousand dollars a year. Surely, kings are coming to the brightness of His rising.

Mamie.—In Persia the year has been full of events in which we have taken a deep and personal interest. God afflicted that land with a sore famine, and, separated as she was from all means of help from neighboring countries, her own government taking advantage of her distress to enrich itself, her people were thrown upon the mercy of the missionaries to save them from starvation. God, to show his love to all, worked through his followers and gave to the perishing without money and without price.

Mollie.—Not only famine, but also war, has been their portion. The wild Koords from the mountains, finding sufficient cause, made war on the people, but through the gratitude of the sheik toward Dr. Cochrane for his professional services, a warm friendship sprang up between these two, so that when the trying time came God's people were protected. The end is not yet. We cannot tell God's purposes in this.

Mamie.—Papal Europe is astir throughout all its borders. France, Spain, Austria, Italy, each is being shaken to its centre in the effort to be free from the slavery of a false religion, which is showing itself to these aroused people in all its horrors; and one of the results of this is the expulsion of the Jesuits from France.

Mollie.—The Jews have claimed a large part of the public attention for a few years past, and have occupied positions of trust. I find that the population has increased in their own lands within a short time to such an extent that in the city of Jerusalem it outnumbers the Mohammedans and Christians together. There are eight millions of them in the world, and they claim pre-eminence in theology, poetry and music.

Mamie.—What will become of this great nation?

Mollie.—They will either be swept away by the huge wave of materialism which has already engulfed many of their brightest minds, or be united under one banner, with God and Jesus Christ as their motto. The various societies for promoting the conversion of the Jews have been able to bring more than twenty thousand proselytes into the fold of Christ since the beginning of this century.

Mamie.—Is there not some encouraging sign concerning them?

Mollie.—Yes, in the last six months, in Hamadan, Persia, forty have been brought to believe the truth. Hamadan is their capital, and it is thought if the Jews of that city become Christians, they will influence all the Jews of Persia. Pray for them, and so all Israel will be saved.

Mamie.—God says, "Listen, O isles, unto me: and hearken, ye people from far." In all this great work have the islands of the sea been overlooked?

Mollie.—Oh no. The Sandwich Islands are called Christian; Madagascar has been given to Christ through the influence of her queen; Australia, New Guinea, New Zealand, New Britain, have all heard of Christ. A native catechist, when told of the serpents and wild beasts and unhealthiness of some of the islands, said, "Hold! are there men there? That will do: where there are men the missionary is bound to go." Truly, the islands are waiting for God's law, and the abundance of the sea shall soon be converted unto him. To all lands God says, "If the Son shall make you free, you shall be free indeed."

Mamie.—Is there nothing we can do? I would not be laggard in the world's work for the Master.

Mollie.—Yes, we can do something.

"If we cannot be the watchman,
  Standing high on Zion's wall,
Pointing out the path to heaven,
  Offering life and peace to all,—
With our prayers and with our bounties
  We can give what Heaven demands;
We can be like faithful Aaron,
  Holding up the prophet's hands."

QUESTIONS ANSWERED FROM THE WORD.

By S. J. Condict.

Little children early seeking
  What to do and where to go—
Is there light to guide their footsteps,
  And a pathway plain to show?

Answer.—"Thy word is a lamp unto my feet and a light unto my path."

Chorus for each verse.—
  Such wondrous words! such precious words!
    Oh may we feel their truth and power!
  Such gracious words! such glorious words!
    Thank God for them in this glad hour!

Little children know so little
  Whom to follow, whom to trust—
Who should lead them, ever faithful,
  Strong and willing, wise and just?

Answer.—"Be ye therefore followers of God as dear children."

Little children are so careless,
  Like the lambs so full of glee—
Will they listen to the Shepherd
  Gently calling, "Follow me"?

Answer.—" My sheep hear my voice, and I know them, and they follow me."

Little children will keep doing
  Things they know are wrong each day,
Sinning often, though so sorry—
  Who will take their sins away?

Answer—" Behold the Lamb of God, which taketh away the sins of the world."

Little children, oft forgetful,
  Are unloving and unkind—
What can sweeten hearts so selfish
  With a love that is divine?

Answer.—" If God so loved us, we ought also to love one another."

Little children, loved and loving,
  Should remember not a few
Live unblessed and unbelieving—
  Cannot such know Christ's love too?

Answer.—" How then shall they call on Him in whom they have not believed? and how shall they believe in Him of whom they have have not heard? and how shall they hear without a preacher? and how shall they preach except they be sent?"

Little children, blest and grateful,
  Glad their light and love to share—
Where shall they the gospel tidings
  Send with faith and earnest prayer?

Answer.—" Go ye into all the world, and preach the gospel to every creature."

Little children, weak and timid,
  Everywhere there's much to do—

Who is faithless? who is fearful?
Hark what Jesus saith to you!

Answer.—"Lo, I am with you always, even unto the end of the world;" "Fear not, little flock; it is your Father's good pleasure to give you the kingdom."

[Tune, "My Sabbath Song," in *Christian Songs.*]

A RESPONSIVE EXERCISE.

Arranged by H. M. J.

[Song or recitation for two children, with Scripture interludes by the whole Band.]

I think, when I read that sweet story of old
  When Jesus was here among men,
How he called little children as lambs to his fold,
  I should like to have been with them then.

Band.—Matt. 18 : 1–5.

I wish that his hands had been placed on my head;
  That his arm had been thrown around me,
That I might have seen his kind look when he said,
  "Let the little ones come unto me."

Band.—Matt. 19 : 13 ; Mark 10 : 16.

Yet still to his footstool in prayer I may go,
  And ask for a share of his love;
And if I thus earnestly seek him below,
  I shall see him and hear him above.

Band.—Prov. 8 : 17 ; Matt. 5 : 8 ; Rev. 22 : 4, 14.

To that beautiful place he has gone to prepare
  For all who are washed and forgiven;

And many dear children are gathering there,
   For of such is the kingdom of heaven.

Band.—John 14 : 2, 3 ; Matt. 19 : 14.

Answer.—
   'Tis a beautiful story the Bible has told,
      And happy the children who know
   The way that leads up to that city of gold,
      And the door Jesus opened below.

Band.—Ps. 89 : 15, 16.

   But what of the children who never have known
      Of this way to the happy land?—
   Who are bowing to idols of wood and of stone
      Which in heathen temples stand?

Band.—Ps. 115 : 4-8.

   They tell me of homes so sad and so drear
      Far over the ocean-wave ;
   No welcome is found for a daughter there,
      Not a flower for a baby's grave.

Band.—Ps. 74 : 20 ; Jer. 10 : 14 ; Rom. 1 : 31.

   Yet Jesus has left the same blessing for them
      Which rests on my own little head :
   Isn't somebody going to tell them of him,
      And all my dear Saviour has said?

Band.—Rom. 10 : 14, 15.

All together.—
   Yes, yes ; we must tell that sweet story of old
      Till all the poor heathen shall know
   Jesus calls little children like lambs to his fold,
      And shows them the way they must go.

Band.—Luke 2 : 10 ; Matt. 4 : 16 ; 28 : 19, 20.

POEMS FOR RECITATION OR SINGING.

FOR FOUR LITTLE GIRLS.

First.— " Jesus loves the little children,
    For he said one day,
  'Let the children come to me;
    Keep them not away.'"

Second.— "There are many little children
    Who have never heard
  Of his love and tenderness,
    Of his holy word."

Third.— " I would tell these little children,
    If they all could hear,
  How he spoke to his disciples
    With the children near."

Fourth.— " Listen now while we repeat it;
    Hark! 'tis very sweet:
  I should think 'twould make the children
    Hasten, him to meet."

All—"Suffer little children to come unto me, and forbid them not, for of such is the kingdom of heaven.

WHAT A LITTLE CHILD CAN DO.

[*Recitation.*]

1. I'm a very little maid;
    I can't do much, 'tis true;

Yet the mission I can aid :
This a little child can do.

2. I can run on busy feet,
Work for mamma all day through ;
What I do for her is sweet :
This a little child can do.

3. I can talk to wicked boys,
Tell them what is good and true,
Make them love the Sunday-school :
This a little child can do.

4. Tracts on missions I can give ;
Send to heathen children too :
Teach them better ways to live
This a little child can do.

5. If *" She hath done what she could '*
Jesus should say to you,
You'd be glad ; I know you would :
This a little child can do.

THE LIGHTHOUSE AND ITS KEEPER.

By George T. Rea.

[*Recitation for a Boy.*]

On a sunken rock in the open sea
Stood a lighthouse high and strong,
And the lamp was there with its splendid flame,
And the keeper, all night long.

But the keeper had naught of pity or love ;
A hard, selfish man was he :
He shaded the lamp, and sent out no light
O'er the dark and perilous sea.

Safe in comfort himself, the mighty ships
    Might strike or go safely by.
"Let them strike or go down; who cares?" said he:
    "Men have only once to die."

One dismal night, by a strong wind driven,
    Came a ship with all sails spread;
No one thought of danger, for no one knew
    Of the sunken rock ahead.

Fast sweeping along came the sail-clad ship;
    The white foam leaped from her prow.
"All's well!" cried the watchman pacing the deck;
    "All's well!" passed from stern to bow.

But scarce died away had the watchman's cry
    When, crash! plunged the ship to her fate;
And there was the beacon that would have saved,
    But 'twas seen, alas! too late.

Oh, fearful cries of the drowning men
    From the seething waves that night!
And they cursed, as they sank, the merciless man
    Who refused his saving light.

The men of the ship are the heathen world;
    The beacon, the book of God;
The keeper, the Christian who shades his lamp,
    And sheds not its light abroad.
—The Children's Record.

CHILDREN'S PRAYER-MEETING IN JAPAN.

By Margaret E. Sangster.

"The dear *little* girls," said the lady,
    In the letter she sent from Japan,
"Take ten minutes out of their play-time
    To pray to the Saviour of man—

To the Saviour who died to redeem them,
   Whose love sheds a light on their way;
They cease from the pleasure of play-time
   For the pleasure of kneeling to pray."

"I heard this all read in a letter,"
   Said Rosa—"'twas sent to mamma --
And I thought of the dark-eyed and slender
   Small maids in that country afar—
Afar over blue rounding waters,
   Where idols are worshiped in dread;
I was glad that the dear little daughters
   Were coming to Jesus, instead

"Of bowing to Buddh, and of living
   Like slaves who have never a thought
Beyond the swift hour of the present
   And the task they in meekness have wrought.
But I wondered how many of *us* girls,
   Whose mothers have taught us to pray,
Ever think of a ten-minute meeting
   In our hour of play-time so gay;

"Or go from the fun and the frolic
   To stand for a moment alone,
And lift up a silent petition
   To Him who is King on the throne;
Who once was a child with his mother,
   And knows just how children can feel;
Who is near us, our strong Elder Brother,
   With grace all our sorrows to heal.

"Dear girls!" said my sweet little Rosa,
   "Dear, precious young girls of Japan!
I think you are teaching a lesson
   That we ought to learn if we can—
To find some time always for praying,
   No matter how cumbered with care,
In working, in resting, obeying
   The Master whose servants we are."

THE CHILDREN'S CRUSADE.

By Margaret J. Preston.

Have you read the wonderful story
  Of what happened so long ago
Away in the Rhenish country,
  In sight of the Alpine snow—

How thousands of little children
  With scallop and staff in hand,
Like Peter the Hermit's pilgrims,
  Set forth for the Holy Land?

From hamlet and town and castle,
  For many and many a day,
These children had seen their fathers
  March to the East away.

" Why do they go?" they questioned
  Of the mothers who watched and wept.
" They go to wrest from the pagan
  The tomb where the dear Lord slept."

And the thought in their young hearts kindled:
  " Let us do as our fathers do;
Let us wear the cross on our shoulder,
  And help in the conquest too.

" The strength of a child is nothing;
  But we'll gather in one strong band,
The strength of ten thousand children,
  For Christ and the Holy Land!"

And so, as they tell, these children
  On their strange, wild mission went;
But the Saviour, who would not lead them
  In the way he had not sent,

Lifted them up in his pity
  (Misguided and yet his own),

And instead of the tomb they sought for,
  Sent them to find his throne.

Now what is the tender lesson
  Wrapped up in the story so?
And what can we learn from the children
  Who perished so long ago?

For the sepulchre's sake where only
  Three days the Redeemer lay
They were willing to face such peril
  As wasted their lives away.

For a temple that is eternal,
  Where the living stones are piled—
(Each stone of the costly building
  The soul of a heathen child)—

Are there ten thousand children
  Over this land so broad
Willing to work, their shoulder
  Wearing the badge of God?

Are there ten thousand children,
  Filled with a zeal intense,
Ready for Christ to offer
  Their labors, their prayers, their pence?

For the gifts and the prayers of the children,
  Gathered in one strong band,
Could conquer the world for Jesus,
  And make it a Holy Land!

THE SAVIOUR'S COMMAND.

Go to the lands afar
Where the changeless winter reigns;
  Night hath her empire there—
  The night of deep despair;

Go bid the morning star
Rise o'er those snowy plains.

Go, love's soft dew to shower
On the far-off southern isles;
Though darkness hath her hour,
Truth is a mighty power;
Go, bid the lily flower
And the Rose of Sharon smile.

Go, where o'er golden sands
The streams of Afric glide;
Bear to those distant lands
The Saviour's sweet commands;
Firm, firm his purpose stands:
"Lo! I am by your side."—*Selected.*

"FREELY YE HAVE RECEIVED, FREELY GIVE."

"Shall I take and take, and never give?"
It was not in the lily to answer "Yea;"
So it drank the dew and sunlight and rain,
And gave out its fragrance day by day.

"Shall I take and take, and never give?"
The robin chirped. "No, that would be wrong;"
So he picked at the berries and flew away,
And poured out his soul in a beautiful song.

"Shall I take and take, and never give?"
The bee in the clover buzzed. "No, ah, no!"
So he gathered the honey and filled his cell,
But 'twas not for himself he labored so.

"Shall I take and take, and never give?"
What answer will *you* make, my little one?
Like the blossom, the bird and the bee, do you say,
"I will not live for myself alone"?

Let the same little hands that are ready to take
   The things that our Father so freely has given,
Be ever as ready to do a kind deed,
   Till love to each other makes earth seem like heaven.

MY MOTHER'S PRAYER.

By Mary Brainard.

I had learned my geography lesson;
   Teacher said I had done very well;
I could say all the capes and the rivers,
   All the capital towns I could tell.

I knew all the countries of Asia,
   From the sea to the distant Japan,
And the isles of the Indian Ocean,
   Sunny Persia and rich Hindustan.

I had learned of the tea and the spices,
   Of the bread-fruit and wide-spreading palm,
Where the song of the bulbul rises
   From the cinnamon-groves and the balm.

But in thought all the time I went farther;
   All the while I was wanting to know
How those dark-visaged children to me would appear
   Should I ever to their countries go.

So I asked my mamma in the evening,
   As she held me a while on her knee;
I shall never forget the sweet lesson
   That she taught in the twilight to me.

She told me those people were heathen,
   Degraded and simple and vile,
Going on through the bondage of darkness
   To the judgment of God all the while.

"We are trying to send them the gospel,
　　For they sit in the shadow of night;
We are asking the dear Lord to help them
　　And to lead them out into the light.

"For you know the dear Lord has commanded
　　That we send this pure gospel to all—
Has promised his help and his presence,
　　And his love to the great and the small."

She said: "In a little time longer
　　All those who now labor to save,
All those who are spreading the gospel,
　　Will lie down to sleep in the grave.

"The girls, who so soon will be women,
　　Must take up the cross and prevail—
Must labor and pray for the heathen,
　　Or the work in those countries will fail."

Then mamma knelt down in the twilight—
　　She was weeping, I plainly could see—
And prayed that the Spirit of Jesus
　　Upon all the dear children might be—

Upon all of the dear little children,
　　Till they grew to be women and men;
And I prayed in my heart, "Jesus, help me!"
　　And I said at the ending "Amen."

A CHILD'S QUESTION.

"How many sisters have I, mamma?"
　　"Only one, my dear;
You have two little brothers—Charlie and Will—
　　And Baby Katie here."

"Then what did the lady mean to day
　　When she looked right into my face,

And said I had many sisters dear
  In some far-off, wicked place?

"They could never know of Jesus' love
  Unless I sent them word,
And that of his wonderful life and death
  They never had even heard.

"I guess she must be mistaken, though;
  For you would surely know
If any such dreadful thing was true,
  And have sent them word long ago."

"Yes, over the waters our sisters wait,
  And well we know it is true
That many perish for lack of help
  That should come from me and you."
—*Heathen Woman's Friend.*

A LITTLE SEED.

A CHILD a penny gave—
  With it one tract was bought:
By this a heathen chief
  Was to the Saviour brought.

A little church he built;
  Men turned from idols cold
Till many hundred souls
  Were gathered in its fold.

How many they shall lead
  In joy with Christ to dwell,
The fruit of this small seed,
  Eternity must tell.

When every little hand
  Shall sow the gospel-seed,
And every little heart
  Shall pray for those in need;

When every little life
　Such fair, bright record shows,—
Then shall the desert bud
　And blossom like the rose.

　　　　　　　　—*Good Times.*

ANNIVERSARY GREETING.

By Mrs. E. B. Day.

We come to-night to greet again
　Our workers tried and true:
God's hand has kept us all these days,
　This happy summer through.

The "Cheerful Workers" we are called;
　We want you all to know it:
If any one has work for us,
　We hope they soon will show it.

For workers dear the harvest's ripe,
　And bending down before us;
We cannot wait if you are slow,
　For Jesus goes before us.

For years we've helped the boys and girls
　In lands beyond the sea
To hear of Jesus, that sweet name
　So dear to you and me.

So now we'll work just anywhere
　That Jesus calls us to;
We're ready, waiting for the work,
　And do it cheerfully.

Now, while *glad welcome* we would say
　To all this Mission-Band,
We humbly look above and pray,
　"God bless our own dear land!"

WE CAN HELP.

I'M a silver quarter.
   Little stitches neat,
And full many an errand
   Run by childish feet,
Earned me very bravely:
   Little girls can do
Noble work for missions
   When they're good and true.

Surely, God will bless us
   With our little all
As into the treasury
   Of the Lord we fall.
Dropping, dropping, dropping—
   Offerings great and small
Dropping, dropping, dropping:
   Hear us as we fall.

COUNTING THE PENNIES.

BY MARGARET J. PRESTON.

AH, what shall I do with my pennies?
   For see, I have such a store!
I never have sold my basket
   Of walnuts so soon before.

How often I've trudged for hours,
   And taken a secret cry
Because I was tired and hungry,
   And nobody cared to buy!

I dreaded to think how mother
   Would look as I came and said

That I hadn't enough of pennies
    To bring her a loaf of bread!—

How Nellie, my little sister,
    Would watch at the door and say,
"I've thought and I've thought of the apple
    You promised to bring all day"!

But now I can fill my basket,
    For there's never a nut behind:
One loaf—two loaves—and a dozen
    Of apples, the sweetest kind;

And a pat of that yellow butter;
    It's dainty and fresh, I know;
How good it will taste to mother!
    And Nellie will like it so.

Five pennies—ten—fifteen—twenty—
    And thirty—and thirty-five;
Just think of it!—here are fifty,
    As certain as I'm alive!

It must have been God who helped me
    To sell off my nuts so soon,
Or else I'd been trudging, trudging,
    The whole of the afternoon.

And now I would like to thank him,
    So kind he has been, so true!
Let's see if I cannot spare him
    A few of my pennies too.

Why, surely I can!—here's forty
    For mother and Nellie—and then,
Dear Jesus, to help thy heathen,
    I give thee the other ten.

WHY DID YOU NOT COME BEFORE?

By Miss Priscilla J. Owens.

[An aged Hindoo woman, on first hearing the gospel, said "Why did you not come before? My hair has grown gray waiting for the good news."]

An aged woman, poor and weak,
She heard the mission-teacher speak;
The slowly-rolling tears came down
Upon her withered features brown:
"What blessed news from yon far shore!
Would I had heard it long before!

"Oh, I have bowed at many a shrine
When youth and health and strength were mine;
How earnestly my soul has striven
To find some gleam of light from heaven!
But all my toil has been in vain:
These gods of stone but mocked my pain.

"A weary pilgrimage I've trod
To win some favor from my god,
And all my jeweled wealth I've laid
Beneath the dark pagoda's shade;
But still the burden on my breast
Bowed head and heart with sore unrest.

"Now, I have waited many a day,
My form is bent, my hair is gray;
But still, the blessed words you bear
Have charmed away my long despair.
Oh, sisters! from your happy shore
Would you had sent to me before!

"Oh, precious is the message sweet
I hear your kindly lips repeat;
It bids me weep for joy again.
My stony eyes were dry with pain;
My weary heart with joy runs o'er:
Ah, had you come to me before!

" How welcome is the glorious name
Of Jesus, who to save me came!
And shall I live when death is past?
And may I all my burdens cast
On him? And is his mercy free?
Not bought with gifts? Such news for me

" Yet, please forgive me when I say
I've needed this so many a day.
In your glad homes did ye not know
How India's tears of sorrow flow?
If you had known on that bright shore,
Surely you would have come before."
—*Methodist Protestant.*

OPENING AND CLOSING RECITATIONS FOR A MISSION-CIRCLE.

By A. W. Alexander.

For all our mercies God be praised,
  And for this pleasant place of meeting:
Kind friends and dear, assembled here,
  The "Little Pilgrims" give you greeting.

It is not much to do for Christ;
  Our talents are not great or many,
Yet what *he* gave he bids *us* bring,
  Nor left the weakest without any.

We are but young, yet we have learned
  That nothing from this duty frees us—
To send the gospel o'er the seas,
  To bring a heathen world to Jesus.

Perhaps I'd better not say more,
  Nor of our plans make further mention,
But ask that what you see and hear
  May now engage your kind attention.

CLOSING.

Kind friends, a moment yet remains
   For me to bid you all good-bye in.
What will *you* do for Jesus' cause?—
   The noblest work to live and die in.

Say not, "So much to do at home!"
   The willing heart shall soon discover,
If we give well, God giveth well—
   Good measure, pressed, and running over.

God speed the day when all the world
   Of small and great shall learn his story!
God bring us all to join the song
   His ransomed people sing in glory!

"TWO CENTS A WEEK, AND A PRAYER."

"Two cents a week, and a prayer,"
   A tiny gift may be,
But it helps to do a wonderful work
   For our sisters across the sea.

"Two cents a week, and a prayer,"
   From our abundant store,—
It was never missed, for its place was filled
   By a Father's gift of more.

"Two cents a week, and a prayer;"
   Perhaps 'twas a sacrifice;
But treasure came from the storehouse above,
   Outweighing by far the price.

"Two cents a week, and a prayer;"
   'Twas the prayer, perhaps, after all,
That the work has done and a blessing brought,
   The gift was so very small.

"Two cents a week, and a prayer,"
　　Freely and heartily given ;
The treasures of earth will all melt away—
　　This is treasure laid up in heaven.

"Two cents a week, and a prayer,"
　　A tiny gift may be,
But it helps to do such wonderful work
　　For our sisters across the sea !
　　　　　　　—*Heathen Woman's Friend.*

LITTLE WORKERS.

By L. A. H. Butler.

[A record of facts.]

All.—Of the happy workers,
　　Youngest ones are we ;
That we're *very* little
　　Any one can see.

Pr'aps you think our help, too,
　　Must be also small,
But we're sure it's better
　　Far than none at all.

Would you know the many
　　Things we've learned to do?
Listen, and the secret
　　We will tell to you.

1.—I made lots of stitches
　　In a patchwork square—
Hardest work I ever
　　Did, too, I declare !

2.—I can't sew, but grandma
　　Holders made for me ;

These I sold to carry
  Light across the sea.

3.—I shelled beans for heathen
  (Papa said I might);
So my little fingers
  Made a shilling bright.

4.—My mamma, to help me,
  Bottled up some ink;
I've sold seventy cents' worth—
  Now, what do you think?

5.—Out of auntie's pansies
  I've picked every weed,
And she's going to give me
  All I'll sell of seed.

6.—I can 'muse the baby
  When he wants to play;
Many a shining penny
  I have made this way.

7.—Sometimes I run errands
  Over 'cross the street—
Earn my mission-money
  Helping older feet.

All.—So you see, though little,
  We've found work to do;
When we said we helped some,
  Don't you think 'twas true?

MISSIONARY PENNIES.

HEAR the pennies dropping, listen as they fall;
Every one for Jesus; he will get them all.

Dropping, dropping ever from each little hand;
'Tis our gift to Jesus from his little band.

Now, while we are little, pennies are our store;
But when we are older, Lord, we'll give thee more.

Though we have not money, we can give him love;
He will own our offering, smiling from above.
—*Sunday-school World.*

THE TWO PENNIES.

Shall I tell you a story, dear children, to-day,
About two little girls, called Susie and May?
They both went to church, and to Sabbath-school too,
And were told about Jesus and what they must do.

One day their papa gave a penny to each,
For he thought in this way a lesson to teach,
And said, "Little maids, now see who'll be wise,
And spend her bright penny for something she'll prize."

Then, hopping and skipping, they hastened away.
'I know what I'll get," said frolicsome May;
"I'll buy some nice candy; come, Susie, you too;"
But, shaking her head, "No, no!" answered Sue;

"For have you forgotten that far, far away
Are dear little girls who cannot e'en pray?
They know not of Jesus, and oh, are so sad,
That I want to do something to make their hearts glad.

"Now my pretty new penny I'll send to them there;
Perhaps it may aid them in learning a prayer.
I know it's but little, a very small mite,
But still, it may help them to learn to do right."

So May got her candy, but soon 'twas all gone,
And she wandered around looking sadly forlorn.
But what of Sue's penny? It sped on its way,
Never stopping its journey by night or by day.

It joined other pennies, and over the sea,
In a land fair and lovely as any can be,
It bore to the children God's message of love,
And taught them of Jesus who came from above.

Now, dear little friends, please tell me, I pray,
Which you think the wiser, Miss Susie or May?
Ah! there's but one voice: "Sue, Susie has won,
For the work of her penny will never be done."
—IOLA, *in Missionary Helper.*

TUMBY.*

BY MRS. W. E. DE RIEMER.

SITTING flat upon the sand,
With a plaintain in each hand,
Tawny face alive with joy,
Tumby, black-eyed Hindoo boy.

Hatless is his oily head,
Round his waist a cloth bright red;
Shoeless are his chubby feet,
Baking in the scorching heat.

Now he picks from tulip tree
Shiny leaf for plate, you see;
Tumby's going to eat his rice—
That's his supper; ain't it nice?

Stars from out the heavens peep:
Tired of play, he wants to sleep.
Archie's mat lies on the floor,
Just before the open door.

Tumby stretches on the mat,
Clasping tight his fingers fat:

* *Tumby* is the Tamil (South India) word for "little brother."

Fast asleep our Hindoo boy,
Full of fun and full of joy.

Can a heathen boy be gay?
Yes, but one thing sad to say:
How to go to heaven some day
Tumby doesn't know the way.

MISSIONARY MUSIC.

1. HAVE you ever brought a penny
    To the missionary-box?—
   A penny which you might have spent
    Like other little folks—
   And when it fell among the rest
    Have you ever heard a ring,
   Like a pleasant sound of welcome
    Which the other pennies sing?

2. This is missionary music,
    And it has a pleasant sound,
   For pennies make a shilling,
    And shillings make a pound;
   And many pounds together
    The gospel news will send,
   Which tells the heathen children
    That the Saviour is their Friend.

3. And oh! what joyous music
    Is the missionary-song
   When it swells from every bosom
    And sounds from every tongue—
   When happy Christian children
    Sing all with one accord
   Of the time when realms of darkness
    Shall be kingdoms of the Lord!

4. But sweeter than the pennies' ring,
   Or songs we love to hear,
  Are children's voices when they **breathe**
   A missionary prayer—
  When they bring the heart-petition
   To the great Redeemer's throne,
  That he will choose the heathen
   And take them for his own.

5. This is the music Jesus taught
   When he was here below;
  This is the music Jesus loves
   To hear in glory now;
  And many a one from heathen lands
   Will reach his heavenly home
  In answer to the children's prayer:
   "O Lord, thy kingdom come!"

6. Then, missionary children,
   Let this music never cease;
  Work on, work on in earnest,
   For the Lord, the Prince of Peace.
  There is praying work and paying **work**
   For every heart and hand,
  Till the missionary chorus
   Shall go forth through all the land.

THE SILVER PLATE.

By Margaret J. Preston.

They passed it along from pew to pew,
And gathered the coins, now fast, now **few**,
That rattled upon it; and every time
Some eager fingers would drop a dime
On the silver plate with a silver sound,
A boy who sat in the aisle looked round

With a wistful face: "Oh, if only he
Had a dime to offer, how glad he'd be!"
He fumbled his pockets, but didn't dare
To hope he should find a penny there;
And much as he searched, when all was done
He hadn't discovered a single one.

He had listened with wide-set, earnest eyes
As the minister, in a plaintive wise,
Had spoken of children all abroad
The world who had never heard of God—
Poor, pitiful pagans, who didn't know,
When they came to die, where their souls would go,
And who shrieked with fear when their mothers made
Them kneel to idol god, afraid
He might eat them up, so fierce and wild
And horrid he seemed to the frightened child.

And the more the minister talked, the more
The boy's heart ached to its inner core;
And the nearer to him the silver plate
Kept coming, the harder seemed his fate
That he hadn't a penny (had that sufficed)
To give, that the heathen might hear of Christ.
But all at once, as the silver sound
Just tinkled beside him, the boy looked round,
And they offered the piled-up plate to him,
And he blushed and his eyes began to swim.

Then bravely turning, as if he knew
There was nothing better that he could do,
He spoke in a voice that held a tear,
"Put the plate on the bench beside me here."
And the plate was placed, for they thought he meant
To empty his pockets of every cent;
But he stood straight up, and he softly put
Right square in the midst of the plate—his foot,
And said with a sob, controlled before,
"*I will give myself—I have nothing more.*"

THE LAST COMMAND.

"Go ye into all the world, and preach the gospel to every creature." Mark 16 : 15.

"Go!"—'tis the Lord's command—
  Leave all your heart holds dear,
Loosen the clasp of the fondest hand,
  And check the burning tear.
Mother and babe and friend—
  Go, while they all remain,
Dragging unto your journey's end
  An ever-lengthening chain.

"Ye"—not some other one
  Whom you deem fitter still;
By you, by you, must the work be done:
  Such is the Master's will;
Nor urge, "There are others here
  By love less fondly tied."
Other hearts cling as close, as dear:
  "Go ye," said the Crucified.

"To all the world," then, go;
  Not to the favored climes
Whose balmy beauty in golden glow
  You have longed for many times;
Not where the nations know
  The Saviour's love sublime,
But where there is dark and godless woe,
  And church-bells never chime.

"Preach" for the Master, then;
  Tell what God speaks within;
Come close to the hearts of heathen men
  Whose souls are soiled with sin.
And let your every deed
  Speak like an earnest word;
Patiently sowing the precious seed,
  Let your voice and life be heard.

"The gospel" you may tell,
  "Glad tidings of great joy;"
God loved poor sinners so well, so well!
  Let this your tongue employ:
How we are saved by grace,
  Through faith in Him who died—
How we may see the Father's face,
  Be blessed, be sanctified.

"To every creature" speak
  The love that wings your soul:
None so wicked, so wild, so weak,
  But Christ can make him whole.
The poor, the sad, the lone,
  The rich, the proud, the great—
For every sinner did Christ atone:
  They perish while they wait.

Go ye to all the world,
  And preach to every one;
The gospel banner must be unfurled
  Wherever shines the sun.
But comfort thou thine heart:
  God only calls his own,
And sendeth forth to the hardest part
  Those nearest to his throne.
—*Missionary Echoes*

THY KINGDOM COME.

Oh, not in vain have saint and page
  "Thy kingdom come" implored—
Oh, not in vain does age to age
  Await thy coming, Lord.

I hear the bells each Sabbath fair,
  How far their raptures run,
And follow through the oceaned air
  The golden tides of sun

To lands beneath the tropic haze,
  Where whispering palms are swaying,
To lands that heard in ancient days
  The morning Memnon playing;

To lands where Night her jewels sets
  O'er deserts fringed with roses,
While slowly o'er the minarets
  The evening shadow closes—

Where prophets toiled 'neath golden wings
  Of temple and of palace—
Where sleep Golconda's jeweled kings
  Beneath the lily's chalice;

To isles o'erswept by frigid breeze,
  And folded deep in mist;
To isles amid the tropic seas
  Of gold and amethyst.

The earth draws nearer to thy breast,
  And thou art drawing near,
And bright in East and bright in West
  Thy coming doth appear.

And sweet as Jubal's chorded shells
  When Sabbath sunshine falls
In notes of multiplying bells,
  Thy voice of mercy calls.

O faithful God! still, still to thee
  We raise the voice of prayer,
Till, circling earth from sea to sea,
  Thy praise shall fill the air.
        —H. H. B., *in Congregationalist.*

THE GREAT FAMINE CRY.

I.

Hark! the wail of heathen nations;
    List! the cry comes back again,
With its solemn, sad reproaching,
    With its piteous refrain:
"We are dying fast of hunger;
    Starving for the bread of life;
Haste! oh, hasten ere we perish—
    Send the messengers of life.

II.

"Send the gospel faster, swifter:
    Ye who dwell in Christian lands,
Reck you not we're dying, dying,
    More in number than the sand?
Heed ye not his words, your Master,
    'Go ye forth to all the world;
Send the gospel faster, faster;
    Let its banner be unfurled.'"

III.

Christian, can you sit in silence
    While this cry fills all the air,
Or content yourself with giving
    Merely what you well can spare?
Will you make your God a beggar,
    When he asks but for his own?
Will you dole him from your treasure
    A poor pittance as a loan?

IV.

Shame! oh, shame! for very blushing
    E'en the sun might veil his face;
Robbing God, ay, of his honor,
    While presuming on his grace!—

Keeping back his richest blessing
  By withholding half the price
Consecrated to his service—
  Perjured, perjured, perjured thrice!

V.

While you dwell in peace and plenty,
  Store and basket running o'er,
Will you cast to these poor pleaders
  Only crumbs upon your floor?
Can you sleep upon your pillow,
  With a heart and soul at rest,
While upon the treacherous billow
  Souls you might have saved are lost?

VI.

Hear ye not the tramp of nations
  Marching on to day of doom—
See them falling, dropping swiftly,
  Like the leaves, into the tomb?
Souls for whom Christ died are dying
  While the ceaseless tramp goes by:
Can you shut your ears, O Christian!
  To their ceaseless moan and cry?

VII.

Hearken! hush your own heart-beating
  While the death-march passeth by;
Tramp, tramp, tramp, the beat of nations,
  Never ceasing, yet they die—
Die unheeded, while you slumber,
  Millions strewing all the way,
Victims of your sloth and slowness—
  Ay, of mine and thine to-day.

VIII.

When the Master comes to meet us,
  For this loss what will he say?

"I was hungered, did ye feed me?
  I asked bread, ye turned away.
I was dying in my prison,
  Ye ne'er came to visit me;"
And swift witnesses those victims
  Standing by will surely be.

IX.

Sound the trumpet, wake God's people
  Walks not Christ amid his flock?
Sits he not against the treasury?
  Shall he stand without and knock—
Knock in vain to come and feast us?
  Open, open, hearts and hands!
And as surely his best blessing
  Shall o'erflow all hearts, all lands.

MISSIONARY WORKERS.

"Little Missionary Workers"
  We have taken for our name,
For we mean to work for Jesus
  And to spread abroad his fame.

Older ones no doubt more wisely
  Act in their appointed lot,
But we think the Lord who sees us
  Kindly says, "Forbid them not."

Chink of pennies is not music
  Sweet as dollars' ring to some,
But the trumpet speaks the tune
  As truly as the mighty drum.

So in Jesus' army sweetness
  Rises to his ears from all
Who from love and gentle pity
  Ring out clear the gospel call.

Each dear friend, will you not aid us
  With warm heart and willing hand?
Then what joy we'll have together
  Working out his last command!

TYPES OF THE SAVIOUR.

WHEN the holy tent I view,
And the shew-bread table too;
When the candlestick for light
Flashes on my wondering sight—
    I behold a Saviour.

Where the perfumed censer swings
O'er the ark with staves and rings—
Ark o'erlaid with choicest gold,
Precious tokens safe to hold—
    I can see a Saviour.

In the crimson blood that flowed
For the debt the guilty owed,
As their sins they each confessed,
With the offering God had blessed—
    I behold my Saviour.

In the holiest place of all,
Where I hear the high priest call
On Jehovah, praying low,
' Save thy people, spare their woe"—
    I can hear my Saviour.

Blessed be the God of might
For the veil, the ark, the light;
For the bread, the blood, the priest,
Types whose meanings ne'er hath ceased!—
    Blessed be the Saviour!

LITTLE FOXES.

Among my tender vines I spy
A little fox named—*By and By.*

Then set upon him, quick, I say,
The swift young hunter—*Right away.*

Around each tender vine I plant
I find the little fox—*I can't.*

Then fast as ever hunter ran
Chase him with bold and brave—*I can.*

No use in trying—lags and whines
This fox among my tender vines.

Then drive him low and drive him high
With this good hunter named—*I'll try.*

Among the vines in my small lot
Creeps in the young fox—*I forgot.*

Then hunt him out and to his den
With—*I will not forget again.*

The little fox that's hidden there
Among my vines is—*I don't care.*

Then let *I'm sorry*—hunter true—
Chase him afar from vines and you.

The fields are all white,
  And the reapers are few;
We children are willing,
  But what can we do
To work for our Lord in his harvest?

Our hands are so small,
    And our words are so weak,
We cannot teach others;
    How, then, shall we seek
To work for our Lord in his harvest?

We'll work by our prayers,
    By the pennies we bring,
By small self-denials—
    The least little thing
May work for our Lord in his harvest.

Until by and by,
    As the years pass at length,
We too may be reapers,
    And go forth in strength
To work for our Lord in his harvest.

GO WORK TO-DAY.

O TOILER in the vineyard!
    Faint not, for thou shalt reap;
Most precious seed thou bearest:
    Then wherefore dost thou weep?

For thou, with joy returning,
    Doubtless shall come again,
Bearing thy sheaves in triumph:
    Thy toil is not in vain.

The day of vineyard-labor
    But brief may prove to be:
A wondrous weight of glory
    Lies in reserve for thee.

Ah! who would idly linger,
    Or from the vineyard stay,
With such a prize before him?
    Let all "go work to-day."

GIVING.

The sun gives ever; so the earth—
What it can give so much 'tis worth:
The ocean gives in many ways—
Gives paths, gives fishes, rivers, bays;
So, too, the air, it gives us breath—
When it stops giving, comes in death.
   Give, give, be always giving;
   Who gives not is not living.
Give strength, give thought, give deeds, give pelf,
Give love, give tears, and give thyself;
   Who gives not is not living.
     The more we give,
     The more we live.

FAITHFUL IN LITTLE.

I cannot do great things for him
  Who did so much for me,
But I should like to show my love,
  Dear Jesus, unto thee:
Faithful in very little things,
  O Saviour, may I be.

There are small things in daily life
  In which I may obey,
And thus may show my love to thee;
  And always—every day—
There are some little loving words
  Which I for thee may say.

There are small crosses I may take,
  Small burdens I may bear,
Small acts of faith and deeds of love,
  Small sorrows I may share;
And little bits of work for thee
  I may do everywhere.

So I ask thee, Lord, to give me grace
   My little place to fill,
That I may ever walk with thee,
   And ever do thy will,
That in each duty, great or small,
   I may be faithful still.

I am a child. It will not do
   An idle life to lead
Because I'm small, with talents few;
   Of me the Lord hath need
Some work or calling to pursue
   Or do some humble deed.

I must be active every hour,
   And do my Maker's will;
If but a ray can paint the flower,
   A raindrop swell the rill,
I know in me there is a power
   Some humble place to fill.

MAKE USE OF ME.

MAKE use of me, my God!
   Let me be not forgot—
A broken vessel cast aside,
   One whom thou needest not.

I am thy creature, Lord,
   And made by hands divine;
And I am part, however mean,
   Of this great world of thine.

All things do serve thee here,
   All creatures, great and small;
Make use of me—of me, my God,
   The weakest of them all.

CHILDREN'S MISSIONARY HYMN.

We are but a band of children,
   Working for the blessed Lord,
Not too small to do his bidding,
   Nor to heed his glorious word.

When he says, "Go tell the people
   Who have never heard my name
That to lift them out of darkness
   Christ, the Lord of glory, came—

"Came that they might say ' Our Father,'
   And that in their sad home lives
Rays of hope and love may enter,
   Such as Jesus' gospel gives,"

So we bring our pennies, asking
   That, like tiny grains of corn,
They may yield a rich soul-harvest
   In the resurrection-morn;

And that some poor heathen children
   Round the throne with us may stand,
Brought there by the prayers and pennies
   Of our little Mission-Band.

"COME OVER AND HELP US."

Through midnight gloom, from Macedon,
The cry of myriads as of one,
The voiceful silence of despair,
Is eloquent in awful prayer—
The soul's exceeding bitter cry:
"Come o'er and help us, or we die."

How mournfully it echoes on!
For half the world is Macedon.

These brethren to their brethren call;
And by the love that loved us all,
And by the whole world's life they cry:
"O ye that live, behold *we* die!"

THE FIVE LOAVES.

By Margaret J. Preston.

WHAT if the little Jewish lad
   That summer day had failed to go
Down to the lake, because he had
   So small a store of loaves to show?

"The press is great," he might have said;
   "For food the thronging people call;
I only have five loaves of bread,
   And what were *they* among them all?"

And back the mother's word might come,
   Her coaxing hand upon his hair:
"Yet go, for they may comfort some
   Among the hungry children there."

So to the lakeside forth he went,
   Bearing the scant supply he had;
And Jesus, with an eye intent
   Through all the crowds, beheld the lad,

And saw the loaves, and blessed them. Then
   Beneath his hand the marvel grew:
He brake, and blessed, and brake again;
   The loaves were neither small nor few;

For, as we know, it came to pass
   That hungry thousands there were fed,
While sitting on the fresh, green grass,
   From that one basketful of bread.

If from his home the lad that day
    His five small loaves had failed to take,
Would Christ have wrought—can any say?—
    That miracle beside the lake?

IN EARTHEN VESSELS.

The Master stood in his garden
    Among the lilies fair,
Which his own right hand had planted
    And trained with tenderest care.

He looked at their snowy blossoms,
    And marked with observant eye
That his flowers were sadly drooping,
    For their leaves were parched and dry.

"My lilies need to be watered,"
    The heavenly Master said;
"Wherein shall I draw it for them,
    And raise each drooping head?"

Close to his feet on the pathway,
    Empty and frail and small,
An earthen vessel was lying
    That seemed of no use at all.

But the Master saw, and raised it
    From the dust in which it lay,
And smiled as he gently whispered,
    "This shall do my work to-day.

"It is but an earthen vessel,
    But it lay so close to me;
It is small, but it is empty;
    That is all it needs to be."

So to the fountain he took it,
    And filled it full to the brim;

How glad was the earthen vessel
  To be of use to him!

He poured forth the living water
  O'er his lilies fair,
Until the vessel was empty,
  And again he filled it there.

He watered the drooping lilies
  Until they revived again;
And the Master saw with pleasure
  That his labor had not been in vain.

His own hand had drawn the water
  Which refreshed the thirsty flowers,
But he used the earthen vessel
  To convey the living showers.

And to itself it whispered,
  As he laid it aside once more,
"Still will I be in his pathway
  Just where I was before.

"Close would I keep to the Master,
  Empty would I remain;
And some day he will use me
  To water his lilies again."—*Selected.*

A MITE SONG.

ONLY a drop in the bucket,
  But every drop will tell;
The bucket would soon be empty
  Without the drops in the well.

Only a poor little penny;
  It was all I had to give;
But as pennies make the dollars,
  It may help some cause to live.

God loveth the cheerful giver,
    Though the gift be poor and small:
What doth he think of his children
    When they never give at all?

THE TWO MITES.

Such a funny thing is told to me,
    And now I tell to you,
What a child as poor as poor can be
    For the missions tried to do.

The story of the widow's *mite*
    Had taught this lesson good:
Each gift is blessed in the dear Lord's sight
    When we have done what we could.

Next Sabbath day said the little child,
    " I've dot *two mice* for you."
'Two mice!" the teacher said, and smiled:
    " What with them can I do?"

" I've brought my own two mice," she said,
    " My *contybution* these;
You said, you know, that with *two mice*
    The dear Lord once was pleased."

Hushed was the rising merriment;
    The two mice soon were sold;
Freely for them the rich ones spent
    Their silver and their gold.

Ah! how they raised and raised the price,
    All for the mission store!
So big a price for two small mice
    Was never paid before.

Thus, sure enough, the gift was blessed,
  The giver's heart made glad;
And so grew "more than all the rest"
  That poor child's "all she had."

THE LITTLE WORKERS.

By Maria A. West.

Little builders all are we,
Builders for eternity;
Children of the Mission-Bands,
Working with our hearts and hands,
Building temples for our King
By the offerings we bring:
Living temples he doth raise,
Filled with life and light and praise.

One by one the stones we lay,
Building slowly day by day;
Building by our love are we
In the lands beyond the sea;
Building by each thought and prayer
For the souls that suffer there;
Building in the Hindu land,
Where the idols are as sand;

Building in vast China, too—
Living temples rise to view;
Building in Japan as well—
Ah, what stories we could tell!
Building on dark Afric's shore,
That there may be slaves no more;
Building in the Turk's doomed land
For Armenia's scattered band.

On Mount Lebanon's fair heights
By our many gathered mites;

Where the Nile's sweet waters pour,
　Building all the wide world o'er;
And one day our eyes shall see,
　In a glad eternity,
"Living stones" we helped to bring
　For the palace of our King.

THE GLEANERS.

We are a little gleaning band;
　We cannot bind the sheaves,
But we can follow those who reap,
　And gather what each leaves.
We are not strong, but Jesus loves
　The weakest of the fold,
And in our feeble efforts proves
　His tenderness untold.

We are not rich; but we can give,
　As we are passing on,
A cup of water in his name
　To some poor, fainting one.
We are not wise, but Christ our Lord
　Revealed to babes his will,
And we are sure from his dear word
　He loves the children still.

We know that with our gathered grain
　Briers and leaves we bring;
Yet since we tried, he smiles the same,
　And takes our offering.
Then let us still hosannas sing,
　As Christ doth conquering come,
Casting our treasures as he brings
　The heathen nations home.

LABORERS TOGETHER.

By Mrs. S. D. Condict.

" We are laborers together with God."

Friends of God! Be up and working,
    In the light!
Plant the seeds of love and duty
    With your might.
God of heaven! aid and bless them
    In the right!
  Give *reward* for earnest toil;
  Give them victory after spoil;
  Give them hope to pierce the veil;
  Give them faith that cannot fail;
  Give a love that changes not;
  Give a zeal with knowledge fraught;
Father, Son and Spirit bless them
    In the right!

Friends of God! The world is waiting
    For the seed!
Lo! within each dreary desert
    Great's the need!
God of promise! aid and bless them
    While they sow!
  Give rich harvest for the toil;
  Bless the seed and bless the soil;
  Pour thy sunshine on the ground;
  Everywhere may showers abound;
  Call the laborer; give the field;
  Count the sheaves and own the yield;
Father, Son and Spirit bless them
    In the work!

THE MISSIONARY DOLL.

A True Story for the Children.

By K. H. J.

"WHAT a very queer dolly!" I hear you exclaim;
"Pray how did it come by such an odd name?
And what possible good could its waxen face do
To Chinese or Choctaw, to Turk or Zulu?"

Well, I'll tell you the tale as it came down to us,
For this dolly had really raised quite a fuss;
And when we all heard how she went on a mission,
We laughed and we cried at this prettiest vision.

A six-year old darling, with eyes full of tears,
Was losing a very dear friend, it appears:
He would tell the poor heathen beyond the great sea
How Jesus our Saviour said, "Come unto me."

And Bright-eyes must show him how dearly she loved;
In some wonderful way her love must be proved.
"Oh, what *can* I give him?" they all heard her say—
"What beautiful plaything to carry away?"

She looked at her treasures with serious thought,
And then she exclaimed, as she found what she sought,
"My new Paris dolly! with bright golden hair,
And eyes that will shut and such fine clothes to wear—

I'll just give him *that* to 'member me by."
But the wise grown-up people said, "Oh, darling, *why?*
Why that is your *very best* dolly, my pet;
Don't give that on which your heart is so set."

What think you she said, this heroic young soul
Who had learned the deep secret of love's sweet control?
"But that's what I *want* him to have," she sobbed low—
"The beautif'lest thing in the world that I know."

" But then," they insisted, "you surely forget
  That gentlemen don't play with dollies, dear pet!
  Pray what would your 'dear Mr. Dale' do with *that*—
  A real grown-up man, who wears a tall hat?"

She pondered a moment, perplexed and distressed,
  And then her eyes brightened with gladness unguessed.
" *He'll want* it," she said, a sweet fancy weaving;
" *He'll* take it—'twill help him to 'muse the poor heathen."

So the love of the darling had conquered at last,
  And her "dear Mr. Dale" held the "dear dolly" fast;
And surely enough a wise prophet was she,
  For it did "'muse the heathen" far over the sea.

THE MISSIONARY CORN.

"Now I think, Katie," Ella said,
  As they their dolls were dressing,
"That our dear Band's the best one made,
  And sure 'twould keep you guessing

"To know how all the money comes
  To teach our heathen Mary,
For truly never to our homes
  Will come a single fairy.

"Can you not guess? Then I must tell
  About the corn we planted.
Six grains to each one's portion fell;
  You see, 'twas what we wanted.

"Each planted hers where falls the shower
  And brightest sunshine lingers,
And watched the leaflets hour by hour
  Come forth like tiny fingers.

"It took so long for them to grow,
  And we in such a hurry,
But mamma said they'd upward go;
  We surely need not worry.

"At last the summer days were o'er,
  Our corn was ripe and golden;
We gathered it, a precious store
  As e'er filled garner olden.

"We put it all together then,
  And got its worth in money,
And so our mite-box filled again;
  Perhaps you'll think it funny.

"But now our heathen girl can read
  The sweet old Bible story,
And learn in paths of right to tread
  With Jesus up to glory."

LILIES OF THE VALLEY.

By M. J. Agnew.

A LILY of the valley!
  Oh, may my nature be
As pure and sweet and lovely
  As that dear flower to me!

A lily in the garden
  Of Jesus Christ my Lord!
May I obtain his pardon,
  And trust him for his word!

A lily that will blossom
  And give out sweet perfume,
In thought and word and action,
  Like loveliest flowers in June;

A lily that will ever
  Be humble, modest, mild;
A ready, willing worker—
  Yes, Jesus' loving child.

Ye lilies of the valley!
  From out your sweet, white bells
Ring music, then, to rally
  The children from the dells

To work with you for Jesus,
  And send the blessed news
That Jesus died to save us
  From all our earthly woes.

BEAUTIFUL THINGS.

Beautiful faces are those that wear—
It matters little if dark or fair—
Whole-souled honesty printed there.

Beautiful eyes are those that show,
Like crystal panes where hearth-fires glow,
Beautiful thoughts that burn below.

Beautiful lips are those whose words
Leap from the heart like songs of birds,
Yet whose utterance prudence girds.

Beautiful hands are those that do
Work that is earnest and brave and true,
Moment by moment, the long day through.

Beautiful feet are those that go
On kindly ministries to and fro—
Down lowliest ways, if God wills it so.

Beautiful shoulders are those that bear
Ceaseless burdens of homely care
With patient grace and daily prayer.

Beautiful lives are those that bless—
Silent rivers of happiness,
Whose hidden fountains but few may guess.

SHOW US THE WAY.

I HEAR a cry from over the sea;
The idol-worshipers call to me:
" 'God is a spirit,' we hear you say;
Where shall we find him? Show us the way."

I hear a voice from the homes of sin
That little children are dwelling in:
" ' He suffered the children to come,' you say;
Where shall we find him? Show us the way."

I hear a voice from the homes of want,
Where the poor are cold in their raiment scant:
" ' He clothes the grass of the field,' you say;
Where shall we find him? Show us the way."

O blind and sinful and weary and poor!
We will gladly show you the open door;
For the Son will lead to the Father's face:
He has gone to prepare us all a place;
And if you hark you shall hear him say,
"Come unto me," for "I am the way."

"OH, LET ME RING THE BELL."

A MISSIONARY far away,
  Beyond the Southern Sea,
Was sitting in his home one day
  With Bible on his knee;

When suddenly he heard a rap
   Upon the chamber door,
And opening there stood a boy
   Of some ten years or more.

He was a bright and happy child,
   With cheeks of ruddy hue,
And eyes that 'neath their lashes smiled
   And glittered like the dew.

He held his little form erect
   In boyish sturdiness,
But on his lips you could detect
   Traces of gentleness.

"Dear sir," he said, in native tongue,
   "I do so want to know
If something for the house of God
   You'd kindly let me do."

"What can you do, my little boy?"
   The missionary said;
And as he spoke he laid his hand
   Upon the youthful head.

Then bashfully, as if afraid
   His secret wish to tell,
The boy in eager accents said,
   "Oh, let me ring the bell.

"Oh, please to let me ring the bell
   For our dear house of prayer;
I'm sure I'll ring it loud and well,
   And I'll be always there."

The missionary kindly looked
   Upon that upturned face,
Where hope and fear and wistfulness,
   United, left their trace.

And gladly did he grant the boon;
  The boy had pleaded well;
And to the eager child he said,
  "Yes, you shall ring the bell."

Oh, what a proud and happy **heart**
  He carried to his home!
And how impatiently he longed
  For Sabbath day to come!

He rang the bell, he went to school,
  The Bible learned to read,
And in his youthful heart they sowed
  The gospel's precious seed.

And now to other heathen lands
  He's gone of Christ to tell;
And yet his first young mission was
  To ring the Sabbath bell.

RECITATION.

Who are they whose little feet,
  Pacing life's dark journey through,
Now have reached that heavenly seat
  They had ever kept in view?

Chorus.—There, to welcome, Jesus waits,
  Gives the crown his followers win:
Lift up your heads, ye golden gates,
  And let the children in.

"I from Greenland's frozen land,"
  "I from India's sultry plain,"
"I from Afric's burning sand,"
  "I from islands of the main."
    Cho.—There, to welcome, Jesus waits, etc.

> "All our earthly journey past,
>   Every tear and pain gone by,
> Here together met at last,
>   At the portal of the sky."
>   *Cho.*—There, to welcome, Jesus waits, etc.

Each the welcome "Come" awaits,
  Conquerors over death and sin;
Lift up your heads, ye golden gates!
  Let the little travelers in.
    Cho.—There, to welcome, Jesus waits, etc.

A CALL FOR CHILDREN.

By J. Lillie Demaray.

Hark to the call that is heard o'er the land,
For children to rise and unite with the band
Of travelers marching in Jesus' great might
To carry to darkened homes God's precious light!
"For children?" you ask. Ah yes, children, for you
With sprightly young bodies and hearts warm and true,
The call is for *you*—our brave women and men
In a few years to come: will you be ready then?

Prepare yourselves now to go eastward and west
Where dear fathers have worked and are now at their rest.
The strongest are wanted, the brightest, the best;
Deny not these callers their thrilling request.
But study and work for the time yet to come,
Then carry to heathen the light of your home.
How precious that message will be, and how bright
To souls who have never yet known God's light!

Each every-day duty perform with your might;
In difficult studies ne'er give up the fight,
Till with God's love your heart, and with knowledge your
      mind,
Is filled; and to him your whole life-work resigned,

How many the youth who now thoughtfully stand
And ponder their calling in this our home-land!
Do you find any better, another more grand,
Than the saving of souls in that far-away land?

REPORT OF CHILDREN'S MISSION-BAND, NEW BOSTON, N. H.

[With some very slight alterations to suit localities, individuals and circumstances, this spirited report will serve admirably for Children's Bands elsewhere.]

GRANDMOTHER BROWN and Grandmother Gray
Met in the cottage just over the way
This afternoon for a social tea.
Grandmother Brown is rheumatic, you see,
And she dearly loves to have Grandma Gray
Come in and chat with her any day.
And to-day, as they cosily sat
Knitting and talking of this and that,
Grandma Gray said, "I must early go,
Because of the Children's Fair, you know."

"The Children's Fair?" said Grandmother Brown
As she laid her gold-rimmed glasses down:
"What is it? Do tell! I want to know
Where other people are glad to go.
You know it is now almost a year
Since pain has kept me a prisoner here."

"Has no one told you?" said Grandma Gray:
"It is strange that I have not, any way,
Since the Band was organized last May.
To the parsonage the children went,
Some of the ladies their presence lent;
They organized as their elders do,
Adopted a constitution too;
Perhaps I can tell it over to you.

First, 'The Ruthians' should be their name,
And, second, it should be their aim
To learn of missions at home and abroad,
And to glean for them along life's road;
Thirdly, their officers should be
A president, vice-, and secretary,
With a treasurer to hold the purse
And all the funds receive and disburse;
Fourthly, any under eighteen could be
Members by paying five cents; and we
Elders could be members honorary
By paying fifteen cents annually.
Eight became members that afternoon,
And others were added very soon;
So now they have eighteen or so—
Good number for this small place, you know.
Once in two weeks they've met together,
And some have come, whate'er the weather.
Five the least number on any day,
And thirteen the largest, so they say."

"Well, well! I declare!" said Grandma Brown;
"There are some wide-awake folks in town.
What did they do at their meetings, pray?"
"Oh, as to that," said Grandmother Gray,
"They had Bible-reading, singing, prayer,
Talked over the missions here and there,
And sewed on a quilt that is novel quite;
It is going to be sold at the fair to-night.
The little girls are going to sing—
Their voices will make the town-hall ring;
Some poems also they will recite:
We really expect a treat to-night."

"A treat, indeed!" said Grandma Brown;
"I wish I were able to go down.
Here, take this dollar and spend for me—
I know what they're working for, you see;

I hope the purses will open all,
And a rich amount in the treasury fall.
Come in and tell me about it, please,
To-morrow, when we can talk with ease."

So, early next morning Grandmother Gray,
As soon as breakfast was out of the way,
Without waiting to rest or sit down,
Ran over to tell dear Grandma Brown
About the " Fair," and its grand success.
" Good-morning," she said ; " you'd never guess
What a real nice time we had last night.
Every one seemed to feel just right;
The hall was trimmed very nicely too ;
The ' Magic Quilt ' was hung in full view ;
The fancy-table was brimming o'er,
Attracting purchasers by the score;
The supper was nice and daintily spread,
From delicious tarts to snow-white bread ;
Then the children dear, their songs and fun
And recitations were finely done;
Our chorister's singing added zest,
And was, as usual, just the best;
Our pastor had written a poem too ;
I hope he will come and read it to you.
Mr. Allen spoke ; and in fact, my friend,
It was a success from beginning to end,
For we made full seventy dollars, you see ;
The children's share over thirty will be.
I wish I could stay and longer chat,
But duties at home will not allow that.
One thing, I am sure, is plain to be seen,
That those who try for the Master to glean
Will find the *handfuls* so easy to win
That many a *sheaf* may be gathered in."

—*Good Times.*

COLLECTION HYMN.

By Mrs. E. B. Day.

To be sung by Six Little Girls.

WE come to ask our Father now
    That eyes be made to see,
And hearts to burn, and lips to say
    " What can I give to thee?"

Chorus (whole Band).—

    We are a Foreign-Mission Band,
        With hearts right brave to do;
    We'll give to Jesus all we can,
        And prove our love is true.

We know we're little, and our store
    Of pennies is but small;
But then we want to give e'en these
    To God, " who giveth all." *Chorus.*

Yet older folks can give thee more,
    Because they've more to give:
This night oh help them from their store
    What is thine own to give. *Chorus.*

Collection. Members of the Band repeat appropriate texts of Scripture, after which the singers sing softly—

    Dear Jesus, may what has been given
        Find some sweet work to do—
    Show some poor soul the way to heaven,
        And help us find it too.

OUR GREAT COMMISSION.

OUR world, our world for Jesus!
    Once more in loving strains
We wake the joyful echoes
    That rang o'er Judah's plains.

Hark! we have glorious tidings,
  And Jesus bids us go;
His message of salvation
  The waiting earth must know.

Hark! what a cry floats westward
  From many an Indian home!
Come hasten to our rescue,
  To dying sinners come.
Not for the gold that glitters
  In mountain-cave or mine;
Not for the bounteous treasure
  Of leafy wood or vine;

But come where souls are thirsting
  While water floweth free;
Where bruised hearts know no **Healer**,
  No sweet-voiced " Come to me."
Have we not passed unheeded
  Their bitter tears and moans,
The wanderer's cry for pardon,
  The prisoner's dying groans?

Haste with the blessed message
  Which drew our souls to God.
The love which Jesus gave us
  Must we not speed abroad,
Till all the world he ransomed
  Shall hear of sin forgiven,
And find the way Christ opened
  Which leads to peace and heaven?

(Tune, " Miriam," *Presbyterian Hymnal*, No. 690.)

THE END.

www.ingramcontent.com/pod-product-compliance
Lightning Source LLC
Chambersburg PA
CBHW020239170426
43202CB00008B/145